PARAM VIR

Major General Ian Cardozo was born in Mumbai and studied at St Xavier's School and College. In July 1954, he joined the Joint Services Wing which later became the National Defence Academy. Here he was the first cadet to win the gold medal for being the best all-round cadet, and the silver medal for being first in order of merit. He was commissioned at the Indian Military Academy into the 1st Battalion the Fifth Gorkha Rifles (FF) in 1958, and was the first officer of the Army to be awarded the Sena Medal for gallantry on a patrol in NEFA in 1960. Wounded in the battle of Sylhet in Bangladesh in 1971, he overcame the handicap of losing a leg and became the first war-disabled officer to be approved for command of an Infantry Battalion, and Brigade. He commanded an Infantry Division in J&K and retired in 1993 from his appointment as Chief of Staff of a Corps in Assam.

Author of *The Sinking of INS-Khukri: Survivor's Stories, Indian VCs of World War I, The Indian Army in World War I 1914-18, 1971: Stories of Grit and Glory, The Life and Times of Lieutenant General Bilimoria, Illustrated Stories of India's Param Vir Chakra Heroes* and *Cartoos Saab: A Soldier's Story of Resilience in Adversity,* he has worked with the Spastics Society of Northern India and was chairman of the Rehabilitation Council of India for nine years. At present he is the Chairman of the 'Centre for Military History and Conflict Studies' at the United Service Institute of India, New Delhi.

OTHER TITLES BY MAJ. GEN. IAN CARDOZO

The Sinking of INS Khukri: What Happened in 1971
Cartoos Saab: A Soldier's Story of Resilience in Adversity
Somnath Sharma: Param Vir Chakra (Graphic story)
Manoj Pandey: Param Vir Chakra (Graphic story)
Major Shaitan Singh: Param Vir Chakra (Graphic story)
Nirmaljit Singh Sekhon: Param Vir Chakra (Graphic story)
Sanjay Kumar: Param Vir Chakra (Graphic story)
Hoshiar Singh: Param Vir Chakra (Graphic story)
Rama Raghoba Rane: Param Vir Chakra (Graphic story)
Vikram Batra: Param Vir Chakra (Graphic story)
Abdul Hamid: Param Vir Chakra (Graphic story)
Bana Singh: Param Vir Chakra (Graphic story)
Ramaswamy Parameswaran: Param Vir Chakra (Graphic story – English and Hindi)
Grenadier Yogender Singh Yadav: Param Vir Chakra (Graphic story)
Arun Khetarpal: Param Vir Chakra (Graphic story)
Piru Singh: Param Vir Chakra (Graphic story)

PARAM VIR
OUR HEROES IN BATTLE

MAJ. GEN. IAN CARDOZO

ROLI

First published in hardback, 2003
This paperback edition first published in 2008
Eighth impression in paperback, 2024

Roli Books Pvt. Ltd.
M-75, Greater Kailash II Market
New Delhi 110 048
Phone: +91 (011) 4068 2000
info@rolibooks.com; www.rolibooks.com
Also at Chennai & Mumbai

Cover Design: Sneha Pamneja

ISBN: 9788174362629

Typeset in Minion by Roli Books Pvt. Ltd

CONTENTS

Dedicated to
The Unknown Soldier

Acknowledgements

I am grateful to the following persons, organisations, and institutions for the help I have received in putting together this story of the Param Vir Chakra and the men who won it. Without their contribution, this book could not have been written. These include authors of books, regimental histories, search engines on the Internet, articles in newspapers and magazines, letters from officers and friends of the awardees, interviews with those who were part of some of the campaigns and battles, and persons, military and civil, whose advice has been invaluable.

To Commanding Officers of battalions and Commandants of Regimental Centres who took time off from their busy schedules, I offer my special thanks and also to civilian persons of Bharat Rakshak and Google.com who have taken so much trouble to put together accounts of a military nature including information on the Param Vir Chakra. Listed below are sources of information which have helped in putting together this story, and whose help I wish to acknowledge.

Commandants of Regimental Centres and Commanding Officers of Units

For citations, photographs, accounts of battles, and personal narratives of the Param Vir Chakra awardees:

Brigadier P.K. Saxena, Commandant Kumaon Regimental Centre

Brigadier Vijay Aga, Commandant HQ Bombay Engineering Group and Centre

Brigadier Kamal Sood, Commandant 14 Gorkha Training Centre

Colonel T.P.S. Gill, Officiating Commandant Sikh Regimental Centre

Colonel S.S. Ghosh, Deputy Commandant Brigade of the Guards Regimental Centre

Colonel Jasbir Singh and Colonel Y.K. Joshi, VrC, Commanding Officers of 13 Jammu and Kashmir Rifles

Colonel R.V. Kanetkar, Commandant the Poona Horse

Colonel Satish Dua, Commanding Officer 8 Jammu and Kashmir Light Infantry

Colonel P.D. Hallur, Commanding Officer 8 Mahar

Colonel Mam Raj Singh, SM, Commanding Officer 5 Mahar.

Colonel Lalit Kumar Rai, VrC, and Lieutenant Colonel A. Asthana, Commanding Officers 1/11Gorkha Rifles

Colonel Vijay Pal, Commanding Officer 6 Rajputana Rifles

Colonel Devendra Kapoor, Commanding Officer 4 Guards

Colonel Anurag Gupta, Commanding Officer 4 Mechanized Infantry, (1 Sikh)

Major Gautam Kalita, Officiating Commanding Officer, 14 Guards

Colonel A.R. Samuel, Commanding Officer 3 Mechanized Infantry, (1/8 Gorkha Rifles)

Colonel B.B. Patnaik, Commanding Officer, 3 Grenadiers

Lieutenant Colonel Ashok Kumar, Second-in-Command, 4 Grenadiers

Lieutenant Colonel Sanjeev Bhatti, SM, SC, Grenadiers Regimental Centre

Contributions from other Officers / Sources

Lieutenant General R.S. Khalon PVSM, VSM, AVSM

Lieutenant General Surendranath Sharma, PVSM, AVSM, Corps of Engineers

Lieutenant General Y.K. Mehta, AVSM, Commandant Indian Military Academy

Major Ashok Nath, Stockholm, Sweden
Major General N.S. Pathania, VSM, General Officer Commanding
    25 Infantry Division
Major General Farad Bhatti
Military Secretaries Branch, Army Headquarters
Mrs Gopal Rao
Air Vice-Marshal S.S. Malhotra
Mr Pushpinder Singh
Squadron Leader Rana Chinna, United Service Institution of
    India
Brigadier Satish Kumar Issar, VSM, the Kumaon Regiment
Group Captain A.K. Sachdev, Research Fellow, Institute of
    Defence Studies and Analysis
Lieutenant Colonel N.J. George, Adjutant, Indian Military
    Academy
Lieutenant Colonel Dhan Singh Thapa, PVC, 1/8 Gorkha Rifles
Major K.S. Mehra, Adjutant, Kumaon Regimental Centre
Lieutenant General Y. Tomar, PVSM, the Grenadier Regiment
Lieutenant General Ved Airy, PVSM, MVC, the Grenadier
    Regiment
Captain Gautam Rajrishi, Adjutant, Kumaon Regimental Centre
Air Commodore R.V. Phadke, Senior Fellow, Institute of
    Defence Studies and Analysis
Havildar Yogender Singh Yadav, PVC, 18 Grenadiers
Mr Sunil Rawat, HRD Executive
Mrs Gayatri Ramachandran
Mrs Shobita Asthana
Mr R. P. Nailwal
The Gurkha Museum, Winchester U.K.
The 5th Royal Gurkha Rifles Association (Frontier Force) U.K.

I would like to thank Roli Books, my publishers for
commissioning me to do this book. I have always desired to
bring the Army closer to the citizens of India. My publishers
provided me with that opportunity.

    Last but not least I would like to thank my wife Priscilla
for her encouragement, understanding and patience during the
last two years when this book took over our lives.

Preface

> *A true soldier does not argue as he marches, how success*
> *is going to be ultimately achieved. But he is confident that*
> *if he only plays his humble part well, somehow or other*
> *the battle will be won. It is in that spirit that every one*
> *of us should act. It is not given to us to know the future.*
> *But it is given to every one of us to know how to do our*
> *own part well.*
>
> *– Mahatma Gandhi*

The Param Vir Chakra was instituted in January 1950, approximately two and a half years after India became independent. During the last seventy-two years, twenty-one individuals of the armed forces have won this award—the country's highest award for bravery in the face of the enemy. Most of them have made the ultimate sacrifice. Fourteen of them have been posthumous.

This book is an attempt to put together an account of these heroes. It is hoped that by doing so, the citizens of our great nation come closer to the members of the armed forces, and become aware of what they do to ensure the security of the nation.

It needs to be remembered, however, that these icons of courage represent a mere fraction of equally inspiring deeds of dedication and heroism by the 'Unknown Soldier' who remains unsung and unrecognised and who has given and continues to give his 'all' so that we, the citizens of India, can sleep in peace.

The acts of gallantry and sacrifice made by the 'bravest of the brave' in defending the nation provide the best example for present and future generations. What is it that makes these intrepid warriors do what they have done? Are they ordinary mortals who have performed extraordinarily well in challenging circumstances, or are they extraordinary persons the likes of whom are rare to come by? These are questions that are difficult to answer and the reader will have to come to his own conclusions after going through the book.

It would be inappropriate and out of context, however, to give the reader descriptions of these amazing deeds of courage of our national heroes without a small background of the war in which they fought. Difficult though it is, to paraphrase the history of a war, an attempt has been made to give the reader the bare minimum outline, so that a link is maintained between campaign, battle and citation. An endeavour has also been made to put together the life sketch of the individual so that the reader has an opportunity to discover what were the qualities of leadership, character and personality that made these men of courage do what they did.

A Bibliography has been given at the end of this book, for those who want to know more about the wars India has fought since Independence and the evolution of medals of honour in India.

Ian Cardozo, 2003

Introduction

The Evolution of Gallantry Awards in India

Awards for gallantry are synonymous with honour, and from the earliest times, societies have given a place of eminence to those who displayed bravery and courage on the battlefield.

Soldiers, the world over, also place courage on the battlefield high on their priorities and those who win such awards do appreciate the acknowledgement of their deeds of valour by some symbol that gives them recognition in the eyes of their peers.

The system for awards for bravery on the battlefield has an interesting history and it is worthwhile knowing how it developed.

Ancient India

In ancient India, the emphasis was on heavenly rewards, and the merit of dying as a martyr in the cause of *dharma* (truth) was long acknowledged as a sure way to heaven. Death on the battlefield was considered glorious, and the attainment of *Svarga* (heaven) through death in battle very praiseworthy.

The *Raghuvamsa*, a work attributed to the Gupta period, describes the ascent of soldiers who die in battle to heaven, accompanied by nymphs. This concept later gave rise to the institutions of *Virakals*, i.e., memorials to the brave, widely seen in early times in southern India. These memorials came into being around the 2nd century and are mentioned in Sangam literature. When a brave soldier died in battle his compatriots marked the spot by placing a large stone bearing his name with an account of his act of courage. The custom survived in Tamil Nadu and Karnataka till the 10th century.

The pleasures of the earth also provided an equally great incentive to the gallant. Sri Krishna in his exhortation to Arjuna to fight, points out to him that in the event of success, the enjoyments of the earth would accrue to him. Warriors who broke the enemy array or saved the collapse of their own front were entitled to royal treatment. Good performance on the battlefield was acknowledged and rewarded by the king with titles, a privileged place in society, promotion and tangible awards of gifts of *jagirs* (land), cash awards, jewellery that included gold headbands, anklets, bangles and necklaces which emphasised that the wearer was someone 'special'. Strangely enough, ancient Greece and Rome also honoured their brave soldiers with similar metal badges of honour, and headbands. Their designs incorporated the use of oak and laurel leaves.

The *Arthasastra* of Kautilya gives a specific and detailed account of gallantry awards for various gallant acts. Some of these are—a hundred thousand *panas* (ancient currency) for slaying the enemy king, fifty thousand for slaying the commander-in-chief or heir apparent, ten thousand for slaying a chief and five thousand for destroying an elephant or chariot. In the *Agni Purana*, an almost similar account is given and the *Sukraniti* enjoins rulers to give due reward to soldiers for their gallant deeds in the form of wealth and power. The *Arthasastra* also refers to a village that was granted total exemption from land revenue for contributions made by its inhabitants to the

State's war effort .The Andhra king, Sri Pulamavi, granted large fiefs to his military officers. King Harsha of Thanesvar also honoured his officers by making land grants to them.

In the *Brihatsamhita* of Varahamihira, there is reference to a band or fillet of gold granted by the king to his brave subjects. It was an inch-broad strap worn around the head in the form of a crown. In the art of Ajanta many men-in-arms are exhibited as wearing these bands. The Hoysala records note the grant of rent-free lands called *kalnad* to the families of soldiers who died in battle. The epics also underlined the need of granting pensions to the widows of these warriors who laid down their lives on the battlefield. It is also interesting to note that a Hoysala ruler in recognition of skilful archery by an enemy warrior conferred on him the title of '*Subhata*' i.e., crown of a good warrior.

The Medieval Period

During the Mughal rule, no medals, badges or decorations as we conceive them today, were given. Indeed, for the common soldier there was rarely any reward at all, regardless of his valour or achievement—survival and plunder were probably enough. However, for the officers and nobles there were titles, robes of honour, gifts, kettledrums, standards and ensigns. A title generally denoted either the quality of a person or the office held by him. Khan was the most commonly used title during the Mughal period: Zafar Khan (Lord of Victory), Shujjat Khan (Lord of Bravery) etc. The Afghan King, Sher Shah Suri had earlier been awarded the title of Sher Khan for having killed a tiger.

The East India Company and the British Period

The history of present day medals is traceable to the days of the Company rule in India. For rewards of intrinsic value, the Company reverted to English practice and began as early as

1668 to reward first European and then Indian officers, for services to the Company, with the issue of specially struck unique gold medals. In 1795, Indian officers were awarded gold medals for valourous achievements. The first being Subedar Abdul Kader, 5th Madras Native Infantry, who was awarded a gold medal and chain inscribed *'For Conduct and Courage on All Occasions'*. For men, however, the awards were 'in kind', e.g., in 1680, four Indian subordinate officers were each awarded scarves, cloth and monetary awards for a feast. In 1809, Subedar Major Muhammad Sarwar, 1st Light Cavalry was awarded a drum, palanquin, sword, horse and the title 'Khan Bahadur Nadir Jang'.

In May 1766, a group of European officers stationed in Monghyr mutinied and a force of Indian soldiers had to be sent to restore order and to arrest the mutineers. To reward their services, the Indian soldiers were given special medals in gold for the officers and in silver for the other ranks. In 1799, the Company struck medals in gold, silver-gilt, silver, bronzed copper and tin for the defeat of Tipu Sultan at Seringapatam.

In 1834, the Governor, Lord William Bentick instituted a unique award for gallantry which was the 'Order of Merit' for outstanding acts of bravery. On performing subsequent acts of bravery, a soldier could be promoted from the 'Third' to the 'Second' and finally to the 'First' class for further acts of valour. This was renamed the 'Indian Order of Merit' (IOM) in 1902. In a unique case, Subedar Kishenbir Nagarkoti of the 1st Battalion the 5th Royal Gorkha Rifles (Frontier Force) was awarded a gold bar to the Indian Order of Merit for winning it 'four times'. The award of the IOM to this individual is of particular significance when one realises that the Victoria Cross which was created in 1856 was not extended to be won by an Indian till 1911! The Indian Order of Merit, therefore, was at that time, the equivalent of the Victoria Cross and the most coveted gallantry award for an Indian, followed by the Indian Distinguished Service Medal, which was instituted in 1907.

Modern India (British Period)

About the middle of the 19th century, the custom of rewarding individual acts of extraordinary gallantry came into vogue in Britain. The Victoria Cross, the most coveted of all British decorations was instituted in 1856 to honour the gallant acts of British soldiery in the Crimean War. The cross consists of a Maltese cross of bronze made from the metal taken from two cannons captured from the Russians at Sebastopol. The royal crest is in the centre of the medal with a scroll underneath bearing the words '*For Valour*'. On the reverse side of the cross is the date of the act of bravery, while the name of the recipient is engraved on the back of the clasp.

During World Wars I and II 40 Indians were awarded the Victoria Cross. Of these twelve were from Nepal. A list of Indian winners of the Victoria Cross is provided at Annexure VI.

During World War I, the practice of award of decorations, based on English traditions, began to become class-based with the Distinguished Service Order (DSO) being awarded to senior officers, the Military Cross (MC), to junior officers, and later on in 1944, the Military Medal (MM) to enlisted men. The Indian Order of Merit was progressively sidelined, reduced to two classes in 1911, and to a single class in 1944. A write-up on the Indian Order of Merit is provided at Annexure IV.

Independent India

As Independence approached, problems seemed to loom for Indian military awards. British rule came to an end on 14 August 1947 and with it also ended the old institution of British honours and awards. Constitutional problems now arose that became difficult to resolve. During the dominion, 1947–1950, the British king remained, in theory, the Head of State. Yet, as the self-governing dominions of India and Pakistan initiated their independence by armed conflict, the issue of awards became a problem. Prime Minister Jawaharlal Nehru realised that, if they were to have maximum value, gallantry awards for the conflict in Jammu and Kashmir had to be given as close as possible to the time of action. And, yet, there were no available awards. In theory, the pre-1947 awards could have been awarded, but the idea of awarding personnel of opposing forces with the same award for bravery against each other seemed quite ridiculous and was rejected both by New Delhi and London. New awards had to be instituted. On the basis of proposals already finalised by early May 1948, the new awards, known as the Param Vir Chakra, Mahavir Chakra, and Vir Chakra were finalised in June 1948. The Governor General of India could not institute the awards as long as India remained a dominion. A draft of the Royal warrant was therefore forwarded in accordance with the prescribed procedure to London for approval of the Crown.

Although our High Commissioner, Mr Krishna Menon, pursued the matter from time to time, it became clear by the middle of 1948 that the king's approval was not likely to be forthcoming. The problems were genuine. How could the king sanction awards for a war between two members of the Commonwealth? Also, the king would have not even a symbolic presence on these medals. The draft warrants therefore were never implemented. With the ceasefire in Jammu and Kashmir having come into force from 1 January 1949, time was running out for honouring the war heroes of the 1947–48 war in Jammu and Kashmir. The prime minister therefore, proposed to Governor General Rajagopalachari that 'His Excellency might approve the institution of the proposed award as our own.' Rajaji felt that having sought the king's approval and not obtaining it, it would be inappropriate for the Governor General to institute awards on his own while India was still a dominion. He therefore suggested to Nehru that since India was to become a republic on 26 January 1950, it would be more appropriate to announce on that day the institution of these awards but with retroactive effect from 15 August 1947. Along with such a notification, the names of those selected for the awards could also be announced. The prime minister accepted the suggestion.

The ideology of the freedom struggle played an important part in independent India's new awards. Unlike the old British awards, the Indian awards had no rank-determined boundaries. No longer would there be one set of awards for the officers, and one for the men. This was in keeping with India's constitution and her quest for social equality. The 'Chakra' series of awards were graded only to degrees of gallantry, not on a stratified class system. There would be no rank dimension to the decorations. In due course, new honours and awards were instituted to honour Indian armed forces personnel. The Ashoka Chakra series followed. This group of awards was meant for gallantry other than in the face of the enemy. A comparison between the old British and the new Indian pattern of awards would indicate a likeness in the two systems with the ParamVir Chakra being equivalent to the Victoria Cross, and the Indian Order of Merit, the Vir Chakra to the Military Cross, the Ashoka Chakra to the George Cross, the Kirti Chakra to the Albert Medal, the Shaurya Chakra to the George Medal, and the Sena Medal to the Military Medal. It is difficult to find an equation for the MVE, if it is at all desirable. The closet perhaps is the DSO except that the DSO is rank based whereas the award of the MVC is not. The first batch of the Chakra series was promulgated on 26 January 1950 and was made effective with retroactive effect from 15 August 1947 to meet the needs of the war in Jammu and Kashmir. The institution of gallantry awards by date is as given below:

1950 The Param Vir Chakra, Maha Vir Chakra, and Vir Chakra
1952 The Ashoka Chakra, in three classes for non-combat gallantry for military and civilians alike

1960 The Sena Medal, Nao Sena Medal, and the Vayu Sena
      Medal for conjoined gallantry and distinguished service
      in the three branches of the armed forces

The Ribbons

Ribbons are integral to the structure of medals and decorations.
Ribbons worn on the chest of a soldier reflect to a great extent
the spectrum of his service life. It could indicate gallantry
awards won, if any, the wars/campaigns he has taken part in,
whether he was wounded in battle, his length of service and
even at times his conduct as a soldier. The custom of using
ribbons for medals is again a British practice dating back to
the 16th century.

Colours of ribbons have their own significance. Colour and
design could have a relation to the country, campaign/war, act
of courage for which it is given. To illustrate the point, the
purple ribbon of the PVC even when worn without the medal
would indicate that the wearer has earned India's highest award
for most conspicuous bravery in the presence of the enemy.
The Victoria Cross, the highest British military decoration
for bravery in the face of the enemy has a crimson ribbon. A
ribbon usually has a combination of meaningful colours on silk.
Saffron, green, blue, white, red, are the most commonly used
colours on Indian ribbons. Of these, red stands for courage and
bravery, saffron for self-effacement and dedicated service, green
for growth and auspiciousness, white for glory and purity and
blue for devotion and sacrifice. Red also symbolises the colour
of the Indian Army, dark blue the colour of the Indian Navy,
and sky blue the colour of the Indian Air Force. Stripes on
decorations denote the category/class of the award. Ribbons
are worn on the left breast in a specified sequence. First come
awards and decorations in their own specified sequence. These
are followed by ribbons that denote wars and campaigns, and
last of all come ribbons that celebrate an event or an occasion,
or length of service.

Param Vir Chakra

The Design

The Param Vir Chakra, as its name implies, is India's highest award for valour in combat. Only an act of the most conspicuous bravery, daring, valour or self-sacrifice in the face of the enemy merits the award. Since its institution by the President of India, on 26 January 1950, only 21 defence personnel have so far been given this award. The decoration is also awarded posthumously. Strict adherence to the above criteria has ensured that the Param Vir Chakra is awarded only to the 'bravest of the brave'. The criteria for this award are so high that of the 21 awards conferred so far, 14 have been posthumous.

The award is presented by the President of India to the recipient, or his widow or to a member of his family, if he is deceased. Officers and men and women of all ranks of the armed forces are eligible for the award.

The medal is of bronze and is circular in shape. On its obverse are four replicas of the God Indra's *Vajra* (thunderbolt) with the State emblem including the motto embossed in the centre. On its reverse, the words '*Param Vir Chakra*' are embossed both in Hindi and in English with two lotus flowers between the words. The medal is required to be suspended from the left breast by a plain purple-coloured ribbon, one and a quarter inch in width. Should a recipient be awarded the Param Vir Chakra a second time, a bar will be attached to the ribbon by which the Chakra is suspended. When the ribbon is worn alone, a replica of Indra's *Vajra* in miniature shall be added to the ribbon for every bar awarded.

The choice of *Vajra* to serve as the motif for the Param Vir Chakra was an appropriate one. It was the *Amoga Astra* (unfailing weapon) used by Indra to kill Vitra, the demon of drought, to release life-giving waters for the benefit of mankind. In Puranic literature, it is said, that this *Vajra* was made of the *asthis* (bones) of Dadhici, a sage of high attainments, for the benefit of the world.

The Ashokan lions (the State symbol) in the centre of the four replicas of Indra's *Vajra* face the four directions and are Buddhist in significance. They symbolise the universal application of the Dharma comprehending all the four directions i.e., east, west, north, and south.

The choice of purple as the colour for the ribbon for the Param Vir Chakra also has its significance. Purple is a combination of Army (red), Navy (blue), and Air Force (blue). It is also the colour of the heart.

Detailed regulations concerning the award as laid down by a Government of India Gazette Notification are provided at Annexure I.

Param Vir Chakra

The Designer

The Param Vir Chakra, India's highest award for valour in battle was designed by a woman! Savitri Khanolkar, later known as Savitri Bai, was asked soon after Independence by the Adjutant General, Major General Hira Lal Atal, to design India's highest award for bravery in combat. Major General Atal was given the responsibility for creating and naming independent India's new military decorations. His reasons for choosing Mrs Khanolkar were her deep and intimate knowledge of Indian mythology, Sanskrit, and Vedanta which he hoped would give the design a truly Indian ethos. She was a painter and an artist, and the wife of Major General Khanolkar, a serving officer. In his opinion, Mrs Khanolkar's military association, her passion for Indian mythology, and her talent as an artist made her the ideal choice. What she designed was truly remarkable.

What is more remarkable is that Savitri Bai was not an Indian by birth. She was born Eva Yvonne Linda Maday-de-Maros in Switzerland on 20 July 1913, to a Russian mother and a Hungarian father. From early childhood Eva was fascinated by India and all things Indian. She was an attractive outdoor girl with a love for winter sports. In the winter of 1929 while on a skiing holiday at Chamonix she met Vikram Khanolkar, a handsome young Indian cadet from Sandhurst. They fell in love but it took them more than two years to overcome parental opposition. Eva came to India in 1932, converted to Hinduism, and married Vikram Khanolkar, by now a smart young Captain of the Sikh Regiment. Fascinated as she was by all things Indian, she quickly absorbed Indian customs and traditions, and the way of life of an Indian army officer's wife. She learnt Hindi and Sanskrit at Patna University and also studied Hindustani music and Kathakali dance which became her absorbing interests. She soon learnt to speak fluent Hindi, Sanskrit and Marathi. She was also a talented artist and made a series of paintings which depicted the basic principles of Hindu philosophy and the ideals of Vedanta. She immersed herself in social work with the Ramakrishna Mission and in the welfare of army jawans and their families. She led a full life, was the first lady to join the North India Flying Club, and learnt Indian classical dance from Uday Shankar. Hindu philosophy became a full blown passion and she delved deep into its intricacies and meanings. She also started writing. Her books include a *Sanskrit Dictionary of Names*; *Saints of Maharashtra*, and two volumes of her as yet unpublished autobiography.

The request to design India's highest award for valour found in her a very whole-hearted response. She took inspiration from the sage Dadhici, the rishi who gave up his body to enable the gods to fashion the deadliest weapon, the *Vajra*, out of his thigh bone which was used by them to vanquish their enemies. She used the design of the double *Vajra*, and on either side of Shivaji's sword 'Bhavani'. Her design was accepted and so was born the Param Vir Chakra.

Little did Savitri Bai ever dream that the first Param Vir Chakra would be awarded to her daughter's brother-in-law, Major Somnath Sharma from the Kumaon Regiment for valour during the 1947–48 Indo-Pakistan war in Kashmir.

Savitri Bai passed away on 26 November 1990.

The Essence of Courage

And how can man die better
Than facing fearful odds,
For the ashes of his fathers,
And the temples of his Gods.

– Macaulay

The fate of a nation during war often depends upon how well men fight and it is said that war has a way of discovering the true nature of men. But to wait for war to know how its soldiers will fight, is to wait too late. By then, the die would already have been cast.

Courage therefore is a matter that deserves the close attention of every thinking soldier, besides others who are responsible for guiding the destinies of nations.

It is difficult, however, to isolate courage as an element for analysis without taking into consideration its catalysts and motivations that cause men to do impossible deeds even at the cost of their own lives.

Questions that need answers are: On what does courage depend and what can a nation do to engender courage among its people and its armed forces? Is it possible in times of peace to predict how individuals will behave in times of war? What are the ingredients of courage? Can courage be judged away from the battlefield at the time of recruitment?

Lord Moran in his book *Anatomy of Courage* says, 'I contend that fortitude in war has its roots in morality; that selection is a search for character and that war itself is but one more test—the supreme and final test if you will—of character. Courage can be judged apart from danger only if the social significance and meaning of courage is known to us, namely that a man of character in peace becomes a man of courage in war. He cannot be selfish in peace and yet be unselfish in war. Character, as

Aristotle taught, is a habit, the daily choice of right instead of wrong; it is a moral quality which grows to maturity in peace and is not suddenly developed on the outbreak of war. For war, in spite of much that we have heard to the contrary, has no power to transform, it merely exaggerates the good and evil that are in us, till it is plain for all to read; it cannot change; it exposes. Man's fate in battle is worked out before the war begins. For his acts in war are dictated not by courage nor by fear, but by conscience, of which war is the final test. The man whose quick conscience is the secret of his success in battle has the same clear-cut feelings about right and wrong before war makes them obvious to all. If you know a man in peace, you know him in war.'

Courage therefore also has social significance because it is desirable that it forms part of the national character. It forms the cement that bonds together the ingredients of national unity which has been our country's strength in times of war. In a democratic set-up men will fight because they are aware that they have a stake in the system, and that the system needs to be protected to ensure the future of the community.

Nations that recruit their officers and soldiers with methods that analyse character, sense of duty, commitment, integrity and self-discipline are more likely to get men of courage, particularly if they weed out those with character defects and instability, rather than nations which make up deficiencies in their cadres by directives to pass candidates in terms of numbers and who do not measure up to the exacting demands that war imposes on individuals. Training systems can improve not only the physical attributes of individuals but can also initiate change in their attitude, behaviour and conduct, provided that the men recruited are of the right sort.

In the matter of recruitment, an important question would be: Is it possible to evaluate boldness and bravery in a potential recruit or cadet? If psychological tests can predict how persons are likely to behave in threatening circumstances, one might perhaps be able to evolve a philosophy or a procedure by which proper selection can be made not only to weed out the unsuitable but also to institute systems that can identify persons with qualities of integrity, self-sacrifice, self-discipline, honour, commitment and personal example—qualities that will make them think and act beyond self and for the good of larger causes and institutions like regiment and country.

In the history of our armed forces there have been many instances where men have performed outstanding acts of courage for the sake of their regiment. To them, it did not matter if they died as long as the honour of the regiment was protected. The regimental spirit of units of the Indian Army and the traditions which nurtured them is the strength of the fighting arms of our Army, particularly in times of war. It is this 'cause', larger than the 'self' that is the ultimate of all motivators that has fortified men against death, and politicians and bureaucrats who meddle with the composition of some of our finest regiments do so only at the peril of the nation's safety.

High morale is another factor that engenders courage, and the strength of a nation and its armed forces lies not in its arsenals but in the attitude of the minds of its leaders, its soldiers and its people. Will power and determination are important adjuncts of courage. It is not so much what is done, but that it is done with full vigour, sense of purpose and the 'will to win'. Battles are won or lost in the minds of men and a lost battle is a battle that is lost in the mind before it is lost on the ground.

Soldiers from rural areas whose communities live close to nature and who suffer the vicissitudes of flood and drought and prowling animals that threaten their crops and their livestock experience danger as part of their daily existence and are likely to be more stoic, obstinate and determined to overcome the trials of war than the city dweller whose daily challenges are less difficult. An independent spirit is part of their nature and also the confidence they have in themselves that they can overcome.

There is also a breed of men who are discontented with

occupations that are not a challenge. They thrive on adventure, and danger excites them as nothing else can. War is just an occasion that beckons them like moths to a candle. They revel in the opportunities that war offers. Fear is common to all men but those who are able to conquer fear more easily, fly high, and their courage and daring are contagious to the men they lead on 'missions impossible' and also inspire millions of Indian citizens into whose homes the media of today are able to project frontline battles.

Kargil was one such war that threw up examples of courage for all the world to see. The odds were all in favour of the enemy and this was just the scenario for some of them to carry out their death-defying missions. The world watched with baited breath as they defiantly dared to do what few mortals could even dream of. They swept us off our feet by their heroic actions and personal courage. We agonised for their safe return. Some returned and some did not. Even the enemy grew to respect these young lions and to acknowledge their courage and daring. The price they paid was heavy. They laid their lives on the line but it was done willingly and without regret. Great acts of courage were performed and not all of them were noticed or rewarded.

An analysis of each of the Param Vir Chakras that have been awarded would reveal in some way the motivating cause in each case. It would be interesting and meaningful if the reader could discern what it was that made the awardee do what he did. Was it the nation's security, honour of the regiment, dedication to duty, self-discipline, love of adventure, concern for one's comrades-in-arms or something else? Notwithstanding the finding, it would be fair to say that the common thread that runs through all of them is character. Character is the key that unlocks all the dangers and tests of war including the final test when one has to sacrifice one's life for what one believes in. And in the ultimate analysis, it is this area that the Army needs to concentrate on, to guarantee high conduct in war.

Can a nation shape the character of its people? I believe it can, if it wishes to do so and considers it important enough. Courage can grow and multiply provided there is good leadership. I also believe that the greatest catalyst of courage is love—love for one's country, love for one's fellow beings, love for the cause and love for the regiment. Christ has said, 'Greater love than this no man has that a man lay down his life for a friend.' In the perception of most people, love may not be a very military word, but in the ultimate analysis, it is on the altar of this word that men and women in uniform make the ultimate sacrifice.

The Unknown Soldier

What is not known to many is that for every act of heroism that is awarded recognition, there are innumerable acts of courage that remain unreported, unrecognised and therefore unknown. This fact is acknowledged by many countries who pay particular importance to this reality and give it great significance at the national level. After World War I, many nations set up memorials to the 'Unknown Soldier' as a tribute to those who had died in combat. As recognition of the sacrifices made by all unidentified casualties in national wars, these memorials are set up in public places where the people of that country are able to pay homage.

In the United Kingdom, the tomb of the unknown soldier is in Westminster Abbey amongst royalty and prominent statesmen who also lie there. But there is one great difference. Whereas one may walk freely across the floor of this historic Abbey, no one may tread on that one particular area which is the tomb of the 'Unknown Soldier'. The boundary of this particular tomb is always marked by flowers, and the British sovereign comes here personally to pay homage to the war-dead and the 'Unknown Soldier' with the rest of the nation.

The most famous American memorial for unidentified soldiers killed in combat is located at the Arlington National Cemetery in Arlington, Virginia. An inscription on the walls of the tomb reads: 'Here rests in honored glory an American soldier, known but to God.' Tribute is paid here by the American public every year on 'Memorial Day.'

The unknown soldier of France lies at the Arc de Triomphe on the Champs-Elysées in Paris, and the people of France gather at the tomb every year on 'Bastille Day' to pay homage. The Belgian unknown soldier lies in a tomb at the base of the Colonnade of Congress in Brussels. The Italian unknown soldier is buried in Rome in front of the monument of King Victor Emmanuel II. In Australia, the memorial on the outskirts of Sydney has been so ingeniously built that the tomb of the 'Unknown Soldier' is lit up by the rays of the sun at the eleventh hour of the eleventh day of the eleventh month each year (Armistice Day). Canada has its tomb of the unknown soldier in front of the National War Memorial at Ottawa.

Most countries of the world have recognised the contribution made by their armed forces to freedom and national security by setting up war memorials for those who died defending their borders. The British in India honoured Indian soldiers who died during World War I by erecting the India Gate in New Delhi, a magnificent monument which has the name of every Indian casualty of the War inscribed on the stone bricks of this edifice. Recently Queen Elizabeth II inaugurated 'Memorial Gates' in honour of soldiers from India, Africa and the Caribbean who fought for Britain in both world wars. In addition, the British War Graves Commission maintains war cemeteries in various parts of India and all over the world. These cemeteries are meticulously maintained and the monument at the cemetery at Kohima has this thought-provoking message inscribed on it:

When you go back
Tell them of us and say,
For your tomorrow
We gave our today.

The institution of a national war memorial was something veterans were clamouring for, for many years but no one paid any notice. Nearly every country in the world had a national war memorial including Bangladesh and Sri Lanka but we did not have one. The poem the '*Unknown Soldier*' in this book, first published in 2003 pleads for a national war memorial. Nearly twenty years later, it was Prime Minister Modi who sanctioned the National War Memorial and inaugurated it at India Gate, amid great rejoicing by the veterans of the Indian Armed Forces and the people of India.

Unfortunately, what has been overlooked is recognition of the Unknown Soldier. Nearly all national war memorials have a place reserved for the Unknown Soldier at, or close by to the national war memorial but in India this is missing. Who therefore is this Unknown Soldier and why does he have to be acknowledged and recognised?

It needs to be understood that during war and conflicts, there are some soldiers whose deeds of daring are acknowledged, but there are many whose courage in battle have not been recognised because they have not been witnessed by someone who could write a citation. Also, there are many whose bodies are blown to bits, whose last rites could not be given and others who nobody knows who they are or where they lie.

The Unknown Soldier of India therefore awaits recognition and a place of honour where he can rest in peace. The poem '*The Unknown Soldier*' says it all.

The Unknown Soldier

I am the unknown soldier, forgotten and ignored
When once the war is over and peace and quiet assured

We fought for you and country and now that we are dead
We rest in quiet exclusion, 'cause nothing more is said
Of how we did our duty, that you may sleep in peace
When once the foe was vanquished, and the strife of war had ceased

The country called upon us to do what needs be done
To oust the vicious enemy and ensure the war was won
Our near and dear ones blessed us and sent us full of pride
To defend our country's honour and some were new-wed brides

We went and fought your battles, most of which we won
Some never came back, all were mothers' sons
Our bodies they do lie there, on hill and vale and plain
Exposed to all the elements of snow and ice and rain

So many were so anxious, some still do wait in vain
What can you do to lessen our loved ones' grief and pain?
Our last rites were not given, we died a soldier's death
Our eldest sons kept waiting, their hopes could not be met

We went and did our duty, we do not ask for much
Only a place of honour, our loved ones' hearts to touch
A place where they can think of happy days gone by
To pray on the lonesome morrow and if need be stand and cry

Although we have left earth's orbit and need to rest in peace
Our souls are not past caring, our pain will never cease
Till you and the country's leaders create a haloed space
For a fitting War Memorial, on valour and honour based.

– Ian Cardozo
New Delhi, 2001

CHAPTER I

THE
WAR IN JAMMU AND KASHMIR
1947–1948

1947–1948
War in Jammu and Kashmir
Battle for the Valley

■

On 3 June 1947 the British announced their plan to partition the subcontinent and informed the princely states that they were free to enter into a federal relationship or political arrangement with successor governments of the two countries. At that time, there were over 600 princely states. Most rulers appreciated the realities of the situation and agreed to merge with the country adjacent to them—India or Pakistan—but a few thought they could remain independent. Maharaja Hari Singh of Jammu and Kashmir was one of them.

As 15 August 1947 approached, Maharaja Hari Singh sought to enter into a 'Standstill Agreement' with both India and Pakistan. While the majority of the population of Jammu and Kashmir was Muslim, the ruler, Maharaja Hari Singh was a Hindu. Pakistan felt that in accordance with the general principles of partition of the subcontinent, the state of Jammu and Kashmir should have come to her. The state had common borders with both India and Pakistan. In early October 1947,

Sheikh Mohammed Abdullah, the leader of the National Conference, the political party with the largest following in the state, appealed to both India and Pakistan not to hustle the state into a premature decision with regard to its future, and to allow time for seeking the peoples' verdict. While the Government of India accepted, Pakistan violated the Standstill Agreement for the maintenance of the *status quo* and enforced an economic blockade by withholding supplies of kerosene, gasoline, food, edible oils and salt.[1]

These actions soured relations between Maharaja Hari Singh and Prime Minister Liaquat Ali Khan of Pakistan. The Maharaja made veiled threats that he would ask for assistance elsewhere if the needs of his state were not met. India meanwhile was grappling with the problems of Partition and was waiting for the state of Jammu and Kashmir to make up its mind in accordance with the Standstill Agreement. Pakistan however appeared to be in no mood to wait for the due process of law to take its normal course and organised an invasion to take matters out of the Maharaja's hands. She collected hordes of tribesmen from the North West Frontier, ex-soldiers, deserters from the State Forces and personnel from the Pakistan Army, supposedly on leave, and all under regular officers of the Pakistan Army. Pakistan attacked Jammu and Kashmir from different directions on 20 October 1947.

The tribesmen were also launched on the Murree-Srinagar Road. Their task was to capture Srinagar. Unhindered loot were the wages they had been promised—loot and women. The force was well supplied with arms, ammunition, rations and medical supplies. It had 300 civilian lorries and enough petrol. It is inconceivable that these arrangements were not made with the full connivance and cooperation of the British civil and military authorities.

Brushing aside the small border garrisons, the force soon reached Muzaffarabad. After looting and burning Muzaffarabad they overran Domel and Uri. The defence of Uri was undertaken

by Brigadier Rajinder Singh and 150 loyal soldiers of the State
Forces of Jammu and Kashmir. Their heroic resistance was of no
avail however against the overwhelming strength of the marauders.
Brigadier Rajinder Singh was killed and the small force annihilated.
Brigadier Rajinder Singh was awarded India's first Maha Vir
Chakra. At Uri, a blown-up bridge delayed the tribesmen for a
while. They reached Baramulla on 26 October 1947. At Baramulla
the force indulged in an orgy of violence, loot and rape. They
now failed to proceed to Srinagar, their given objective. They did
something their Pakistani planners had not foreseen. Many left for
their homes to deposit the loot and the women they had captured
and then to come back for more! This saved Srinagar.

The loss of Domel and Muzaffarabad had by now shaken
the Maharaja. The people, including the officials were terror-
stricken. State officials were leaving their jobs and with the
breakdown of communication he saw his state plunging into
chaos. On 24 October, he appealed to the Government of India
for help. The government of India informed the Maharaja that
it could not lawfully send troops into Jammu and Kashmir
without the Maharaja's accession to the Union of India. The
Maharaja signed the Instrument of Accession on 26 October
1947 with the full support of Sheikh Abdullah, the leader of
the National Conference, the political party with the largest
following in the state, and with this, the state of Jammu and
Kashmir became an integral part of the Union of India—legally,
morally and constitutionally.

Colonel Akbar Khan, Director Weapons and Equipment
at the Pakistan Army Headquarters was placed in charge of
operations. He has left a valuable historical account that gives
details of the role played by senior Pakistani military officers
and key political leaders. Akbar Khan confirms the central role
of Pakistan's Prime Minister, Nawabzada Liaquat Ali Khan and
many others in the attempt to take Jammu and Kashmir by force.

Whereas it is evident that Pakistan's move to annex the
state of Jammu and Kashmir was a premeditated plan prepared

soon after Partition, India had not made any plans for military intervention in the state. It was only on 26 October 1947 that the Indian Army was informed that the state had acceded to India and that emergency action had to be taken to collect the troops and to convey them as quickly as possible to save the beleaguered state.[2]

The most accessible unit in Delhi for moving into the Kashmir Valley was the 1st Battalion the 5th Royal Gorkha Rifles (Frontier Force) which was at the Red Fort on internal security duties. Although an Indian Commanding Officer, Lieutenant Colonel A.S. Pathania, MC had been posted, Indian officers had yet to be posted in. Army Headquarters, therefore, did not permit the unit's induction into Jammu and Kashmir at this stage. The next most accessible unit was 1 Sikh deployed for internal security duties around Gurgaon. The sub-units however were deployed further afield. Lieutenant Colonel Ranjit Rai, the Commanding Officer was ordered to assemble his unit at Gurgaon and to move to Delhi without delay. This unit, in bits and pieces, was first to be flown into Srinagar from Safdarjung air field in civil and military aircraft which were hastily collected by Army Headquarters Movement Control. The Commanding Officer was the first to land at Srinagar airfield on the morning of 27 October 1947. Finding the airfield intact he decided that the defence of Srinagar was best served by going out and halting the enemy advance till more troops arrived.

The raiders meanwhile had reorganised themselves after their orgy of destruction, loot and rape and recommenced their advance on 28 October 1947 along the Baramulla-Srinagar road. 1 Sikh in the meanwhile had occupied a position outside Baramulla. As the raiders approached, the men of the Sikh battalion opened fire and inflicted heavy casualties on them. The raiders however, far outnumbered the Sikhs and Lieutenant Colonel Rai decided to withdraw his force to better defensive ground closer to Srinagar from where he could ensure its security. In the ensuing action, Lieutenant Colonel Rai was killed while evacuating his wounded soldiers.

The Sikh battalion withdrew from the vicinity of Baramulla and occupied defences on high ground at Pattan, about 27 km from Srinagar by the morning of 29 October. The enemy soon made contact with the position and attacked repeatedly but were, however, repelled with serious casualties.

Meanwhile 161 Infantry Brigade started arriving at Srinagar by air from 29 October onwards. The battalions of the brigade were 4 Kumaon, 1 Punjab, and 1 Kumaon (Para). The force was commanded by Brigadier L.P. Sen, DSO (Distinguished Service Order) who has given a graphic account of his brigade's performance in his book *Slender was the Thread*.

4 Kumaon, commenced their 'fly-in' into the valley on 31 October 1947. 'D' Company under Major Somnath Sharma was the first element of 161 Infantry Brigade to arrive.

This now takes us to the story of the Battle of Badgam where Major Somnath Sharma won India's first Param Vir Chakra.

1. *Reported by Mountbatten in his letters to the king, 7 November 1947. Quoted by Stanley Wolpert in* Jinnah of Pakistan *(Oxford University Press, New York 1984. Reprinted by Oxford University Press, Delhi, 1984) and by Lamb, op. cit., p.126.*
2. *The entire sequence of events was first related to C.R. Attlee, Prime Minister of Britain, by Pandit Nehru, in a telegram sent via the UK High Commission in India on 28 October 1947 at 0500 hours. A more detailed version was given in the Government of India's White Paper on the Accession of Kashmir to India, which was released on 22 March 1948. The version of the events given in the above documents remained unaltered throughout the long and tortured debates in the Security Council from 1947 to 1965 and thereafter.*

Major Somnath Sharma, PVC
4 KUMAON

The Battle of Badgam

Elements of 161 Infantry Brigade were sent out to guard the various approaches to Srinagar. In the meanwhile, reports were being received that the raiders were infiltrating towards Srinagar from different routes and that one such force was heading for Badgam, a village about eight miles south-west of Srinagar. The village was less than two miles from the airfield. An enemy force lodged there could easily threaten it.

A force consisting of two companies, 'A' and 'D', of 4 Kumaon, under Major Somnath Sharma, and a company of 1 Para Kumaon under Captain Ronald Wood were sent to Badgam.

Major Somnath Sharma was a seasoned soldier who had seen much of the bitter fighting in the Arakan, in the Burma Campaign of World War II and had already been mentioned-in-despatches. His left arm was heavily plastered, the result of a fracture, sustained in a fall while doing gymnastics.

Although advised to remain behind at Delhi until the fracture had set, and the plaster removed, he had insisted on accompanying his company into the Valley. He had argued that he knew his men better than anyone else, and if they were going into action, they were not going in without him.

The two companies of 4 Kumaon moved towards Badgam, followed after a short interval by the company of 1 Para Kumaon. Soon after first light, Major Sharma reported that he was in position on high ground west of the village of Badgam and had established a firm base there. 1 Para Kumaon had reached a position south-east of the village. The situation was reported as 'quiet and peaceful'. 1 Para Kumaon was then ordered to 'pass through' 4 Kumaon and to head for Magam, to make contact with 1 Punjab and to return to the airfield.

1 Para Kumaon company had an uneventful patrol to Magam, and having made contact with 1 Punjab returned to the airfield just before 1300 hours. Captain Wood reported that there were no signs of the enemy and that the villages skirted en route were undamaged. Major Sharma also reported that all was quiet and peaceful in the village of Badgam. He observed that the villagers were quietly going about their daily chores. He also noticed what he thought was a 'group of villagers' sheltering in a nala.

Major Sharma was ordered to commence thinning out from the Badgam position from 1330 hours. At 1400 hours Major Sharma reported that 'A' company had moved back towards the airfield. The Brigade Commander, Brigadier L. P. Sen, DSO told Major Sharma to hold on to the position for another hour and to commence withdrawal from the position from 1500 hours. Major Sharma confirmed that Badgam continued to be quiet and peaceful. There was no indication whatsoever of what was going to happen within the next 30 minutes.

Half an hour after 'A' company of 4 Kumaon had left, the group of villagers in the nala began to move around and to disperse nonchalantly in different directions around Major Sharma's company. The unsuspecting Kumaonis took this movement to be the normal 'dispersal' of a group of people towards their homes. They had no idea that these were the cunning raiders disguised and posing as Kashmiri villagers with their weapons hidden under their loose cloaks. They were, therefore, taken by surprise when firing commenced from the houses in the village and when a mortar opened up on them followed by light machine gun fire from close range. Faced with fire from the village Major Sharma reported that he was hesitant to return the fire for fear of killing or injuring women and children.

While Major Sharma was reporting the changed situation to the Brigade Commander and how he was coping with it, his company consisting of less than 90 men was attacked by a large force from a depression to the west of his position together with mortar and automatic fire.

Major Somnath Sharma saying goodbye at Safdarjung Airfield with his left hand still in cast.

Major Sharma engaged this new threat with whatever he had. The first attack was repulsed, but enemy pressure began to increase. Major Sharma's company was now facing about 500 tribesmen and was hopelessly outnumbered. He now asked the Brigade for help. The Brigade promised air support. Being very short of men, Major Sharma himself laid out the ground panel indicators to guide the aircraft onto the target.

The nearest airfield that could support this operation was at Srinagar. It was equipped with four Spitfires and two Harvards/ Tempests. The problem was lack of aircraft fuel and no maps of the area. The Brigade had only one map! This map was now required to be shared between the Army and the Air Force. Brigadier Sen solved the problem by cutting out a two-inch square portion of the target area for the aircraft. This little map was used by the first aircraft and the following aircraft took on the same target. Unfortunately, only one run was possible due to lack of aircraft fuel. The two-inch portion of the map that was cut out was later returned to the Brigade Headquarters. It was stuck back on the map which continued to be used for further operations in the 'Valley'.

Under assault from three sides, 'D' Company began to suffer heavy casualties. Outnumbered 7 to 1, Major Sharma did not lose heart. Although the Brigade Headquarter had informed him that 1 Punjab was coming to their aid, he knew that their arrival would take time. With utter disregard for his own safety he moved from one section to another cheering his men and motivating them. The men were greatly inspired by him and continued to make the enemy pay a heavy price by killing as many of them as possible. When he discovered that the casualties were affecting the functioning of the light machine guns, he began to fill the magazines himself. It was while he was so engaged that an enemy mortar shell landed near him killing him on the spot.

Besides Major Sharma, the company lost Subedar Prem Singh Mehta, and 20 other ranks. 26 were wounded. Enemy casualties were heavy. When Badgam was recaptured by our troops the bodies of over 300 tribesmen were counted.

Leadership and gallantry of a very high order was displayed by Major Somnath Sharma and the Government of India responded by awarding him Independent India's highest award for gallantry—India's very first Param Vir Chakra.

* * *

Citation

Major Somnath Sharma
4 KUMAON (IC–521)

On 3 November 1947, Major Somnath Sharma's company was ordered on a fighting patrol to Badgam in the Kashmir Valley. He reached his objective at first light on 3 November and took up a position south of Badgam at 1100 hours. The enemy, estimated at about 500 attacked his company position from three sides, the company began to sustain heavy casualties.

Fully realising the gravity of the situation and the direct threat that would result to both the aerodrome and Srinagar if the enemy attack was not held until reinforcements could be rushed to close the gap leading to Srinagar via Hum

Hom, Major Sharma urged his company to fight the enemy tenaciously. With extreme bravery he kept rushing across the open ground to his sections exposing himself to heavy and accurate fire to urge them to hold on.

Keeping his nerve, he skilfully directed the fire of his sections into the ever-advancing enemy. He repeatedly exposed himself to the full fury of enemy fire and laid out cloth strips to guide our aircraft onto their targets in full view of the enemy.

Realising that casualties had affected the effectiveness of his light automatics, this officer whose left hand was in plaster, personally commenced filling magazines and issuing them to the light machine gunners. A mortar shell landed right in the middle of the ammunition resulting in an explosion that killed him.

Major Sharma's company held on to its position and the remnants withdrew only when almost completely surrounded. His inspiring example resulted in the enemy being delayed for six hours, thus gaining time for our reinforcements to get into position at Hum Hom to stem the tide of the enemy advance.

His leadership, gallantry and tenacious defence were such that his men were inspired to fight the enemy by seven to one, six hours after this gallant officer had been killed.

He has set an example of courage and qualities seldom equalled in the history of the Indian Army. His last message to the Brigade Headquarters a few moments before he was killed was, '*The enemy are only 50 yards from us. We are heavily outnumbered. We are under devastating fire. I shall not withdraw an inch but will fight to the last man and the last round.*'

Gazette of India Notification
No. 2—Press/50

Linkages and Legacies

One man with courage makes a majority.
– Andrew Jackson

They say some leaders are born and some are made. Sometimes young men also grow into leadership if they are in the right environment. Looking at the life of Somnath Sharma, India's first Param Vir Chakra, we see instances that indicate that leadership was ingrained in his character. However it is pertinent to know that he grew up in a family that was very much 'Army' and where qualities of character were nurtured and encouraged. His father, Amarnath Sharma, an Army doctor, could have set up a lucrative practice at Lahore but he preferred to serve Indian soldiers fighting in foreign lands during World War II. What influenced Somnath and his brothers even more was the example of the life and death of their mother's brother, Lieutenant Krishan Datt Vasudeva of the 4/19 Hyderabadis who died fighting the Japanese in Malaya in 1942. In one of his last letters to his parents in December 1941, he said, '. . . I am doing which my duty brings before me. The fear of death is there no doubt, but it vanishes when I think of the teachings of the Lord in the *Gita*. The soul is an ever living thing, so what does it matter if it leaves this body? Please Father, I am not painting a dark picture but let me tell you one thing. If I die here, I can assure you with all my heart that I will die *as a soldier...* and I will have no regrets when I die... May God bless you all.'

Lieutenant K.D. Vasudeva, the MTO (Mechanical Transport Officer) of his battalion was listed as 'missing believed killed'. Somnath Sharma volunteered for the (Hyderabad) Kumaon Regiment mainly because of the inspiring example of his uncle. According to those who knew him, Somnath was a down-to-earth, practical soldier who believed in doing his best in whatever he was asked to do—no theatricals, no frills, and no playing to the gallery. When asked by his Commanding Officer to withdraw from his position because of the overwhelming odds, his answer was that they would fight to the last man and the last round because he knew that it was vital to delay the enemy as otherwise the road to Srinagar lay open. The delay that he and his company imposed on the enemy and the heavy toll they took in terms of casualties achieved just that. The enemy stopped, and had to regroup and reorganise because of the heavy casualties that they suffered. When Badgam was subsequently recaptured the bodies of over 300 raiders were counted, and the delay imposed was sufficient to block the enemy and to allow our own troops to resume the offensive.

Somnath was strong and tough even at school, very good at games and an excellent gymnast. Like most army families, schools were where their father was posted. However, Somnath and his brothers spent their final years at Sherwood, Naini Tal as some stability was necessary at that stage. Somnath's father Amarnath Sharma was commissioned into the Indian Medical Service in 1915 and is probably the only army medical officer who served in virtually every theatre in World War I and that includes the Middle East, the Black Sea, Persia, Turkey and Mesopotamia. Then the North West Frontier and China between the wars, CO of Military Hospital Delhi Cantt., then Libya, the Arakan in Burma, then Indonesia and on to the Islands in the Pacific during World War II; he commanded a hospital in Ceylon, was ADMS Rawalpindi Area, became DDMS Eastern Command in August 1947 and then promoted Director Medical Services Indian Army as a Major General. He is one of the very few army officers who has had the distinction of serving on both the Western and Eastern fronts during World War II. Surendra Nath, better known in army circles as 'Tindy' joined the Corps of Engineers and retired as the Engineer-in-Chief. The youngest brother, Vishwa Nath chose the Armoured Corps and rose to the highest rank possible in the Army, as

Chief of Army Staff. Of the two sisters, Kamla joined the Army as a doctor, like her father. She married Major K.N. Tiwary who rose to the rank of a Major General. Their daughter Lieutenant Colonel Uma Tiwari carries on the tradition of her mother and grandfather as a doctor in the Army Medical Corps. The other sister, Manorama, married an army officer and General Surendra Nath's son, Gautam Shaunik is a Lieutenant Colonel in the Armoured Corps—a very distinguished army family indeed, whose military roots go back to the times of Maharaja Ranjit Singh when an uncle was a 'Tees Hazari' in the Maharaja's army.

Soon after being commissioned, Somnath was fighting the Japanese in the Arakan. Even as a young officer he inspired his troops with his instinctive grasp of leadership and his ability to do the right thing in the right way and at the right time. In one particular action, in the Arakan, he brought back one of his wounded soldiers, carrying him on his back in the midst of heavy enemy fire. For his courage under fire, in the face of the enemy, he was 'mentioned-in-despatches'. He, therefore, was already baptised by fire and christened with an award for bravery, even before he was to fight at the battle of Badgam in Jammu and Kashmir.

For his outstanding performance at the battle of Badgam he was in fact recommended for the award of the Victoria Cross, as at that time, the Chakra series of gallantry awards had not yet been instituted. The country at that time being independent was in the strange situation of not being eligible for the British awards and its own awards had yet to come into being. He was subsequently awarded India's first Param Vir Chakra—India's highest award for bravery in the face of the enemy.

Somnath was just twenty-five and a bachelor when he died. His exemplary leadership in battle has however set the pace and standard for officers of today and tomorrow to follow.

Company Havildar Major Piru Singh

6 RAJPUTANA RIFLES

Prelude to the Battle of Darapari

After the threat to Srinagar was removed, the Indian forces consolidated themselves in the Uri area. The spring of 1948 was thereafter utilised for preparation for a major offensive to rid the Kashmir Valley of the aggressors. Major General Thimayya, DSO was appointed General Officer Commanding Sri Division (19 Infantry Division).

General Thimayya decided to launch his divisional offensive with the main thrust along the Uri-Domel road by 161 Infantry Brigade under Brigadier L.P. Sen, DSO. 163 Infantry Brigade under Brigadier Harbaksh Singh was to carry out a divisionary operation towards Tithwal from Handwara, two or three days earlier, in order to draw as much of the enemy reserve as possible from Muzaffarabad. The Poonch Brigade was to carry out a battalion operation towards Bagh to tie down enemy forces there.

Both brigades commenced operations in the third week of May. Dogarpur, Trehagam and Chokibal were captured against stiff opposition. The advance to Tithwal continued and on 22 May Tithwal was captured. 6 Rajputana Rifles cleared an important hill feature called Darapari. Pakistan could not reconcile itself to the setback suffered in the Tithwal Sector and launched repeated counter-attacks to dislodge the Indians. It was here at the Battle of Darapari, that Company Havildar Major Piru Singh, displayed gallantry of a very high order in defending his position and was awarded the Param Vir Chakra.

The Battle of Darapari

Darapari is a hill feature over 1100 feet high. A narrow crest runs over a series of steep vertical rocky cliffs. The 6th Battalion, the Rajputana Rifles after an arduous march of 30 miles from Tangdhar was sent to capture Darapari for operations in the Tithwal valley. The battalion was told that from intelligence reports it appeared that the enemy had not had enough time to dig-in intensively and therefore could be dislodged by a swift offensive. This information proved to be inaccurate as the enemy defensive position was very strong. The battalion did not have time for proper reconnaissance of the enemy position.

The Commanding Officer gave his orders on the afternoon of 17 July. The approaches to the Darapari position were narrow and deployment for the attack was difficult. Better approaches by distant spurs were not possible due to the constraints of time.

The attack for the capture of Darapari was to take place after the moon had set at 0130 hours on the night of 17/18 July, 1948 to take advantage of the darkness. Company Havildar Major Piru Singh's platoon was leading the assault. The troops reached close to the enemy defences and heavy fire erupted all around them. Subedar Bhika Singh the platoon commander was hit. Seeing this, Company Havildar Major Piru Singh took command and led his gallant platoon against the murderous fire coming from the enemy deployed in well-dug trenches and bunkers on high ground. The enemy medium machine guns had been sited to cover all possible approaches. Three medium machine guns were fixed on this bottleneck. Company Havildar Major Piru Singh led the leading section of his platoon which was met with fire from both flanks and a volley of grenades from the enemy bunkers. Although more than half of his section were killed or wounded, Company Havildar Major Piru Singh did not falter and rushed forward against the nearest enemy medium machine gun position with the battalion battle-cry of *Raja Ramchander ki Jai*. The remainder of the section followed him through the curtain of grenade splinters that tore through them. Company Havildar Major Piru Singh continued to advance without any thought of personal safety or self-protection. Soon he was on top of the gun position blazing away at the gun-crew with his Sten gun. He then jumped into the gun pit bayonetting its crew and silencing one machine-gun. Now, he was the sole survivor of his section, the rest of his men were either dead or disabled. At this juncture an enemy grenade wounded him in the face. With blood dripping from his face, he crawled out of the gun-pit and assaulted the next trench and repeating the battalion battle-cry jumped on the two occupants and bayonetted them to death. As he charged the third trench he was hit in the head and was seen dropping on to the third trench. This was followed almost at once by an explosion in the trench which showed that his last grenade had found its mark. Inspired by his action, the rest of his company followed and Darapari was captured against death-defying odds. Much of the success of the capture of Darapari was due to the inspiring example and superhuman courage of Company Havildar Major Piru Singh.

∗ ∗ ∗

Citation

Company Havildar Major Piru Singh
6ᵀᴴ BATTALION THE RAJPUTANA RIFLES (NO. 2831592)

South of Tithwal, 'D' Company, of which No. 2831592 Piru Singh was Havildar Major, was detailed to attack and capture an enemy occupied hill feature.

The enemy had well dug in positions and had sited his MMGs so as to cover all possible approaches. As the attack advanced, it was met with heavy MMG fire from both flanks. Volleys of grenades were hurled down from enemy bunkers. Company Havildar Major Piru Singh was then with the forward most Section of the company.

Seeing more than half of the Section killed or wounded, he did not lose courage. With battle cries he encouraged the remaining men and rushed forward with great determination onto the nearest enemy MMG position. Grenade splinters ripping his clothes and wounding him at several places, he continued to advance without the least regard for his safety. He was on top of the MMG position wounding the gun crew with Sten gun fire. With complete disregard to his bleeding wounds he made a mad jump on the MMG crew bayoneting them to death, thus silencing the gun.

By then he suddenly realised that he was the sole survivor of the section, the rest of them either dead or wounded. Another grenade thrown at him wounded him in the face. With blood dripping from his face wounds in his eyes, he crawled out of the trench, hurling grenades at the next enemy position.

With a loud battle cry, he jumped on the occupants of the next trench bayonetting two to death. This action was witnessed by the 'C' Company Commander who was directing fire in support of the attacking company.

As Havildar Major Piru Singh emerged out of the second trench to charge on the 3rd enemy bunker, he was hit in the head by a bullet and was seen dropping on the edge of the enemy trench. There was an explosion in the trench, which showed that his grenade had done its work. By then Company Havildar Major Piru Singh's wounds had proved fatal.

He had paid with his life for his singularly brave act, but he had left for the rest of his comrades an unique example of single-handed bravery and determined cold courage.

Gazette of India Notification
No. 8—Press/52

* * *

Rustic Youth to National Hero

Courage consists not in hazarding without fear, but being resolutely minded in a just cause. The brave is not he who feels no fear, for that were stupid and irrational, but he whose noble soul subdues its fear and bravely dares the danger nature shrinks from.

– Ferrold

Piru Singh came from an agricultural family of the warrior clan of the Rajputs of the village of Beri in Jhunjhunu district in Rajasthan. He was born in May 1918 and was one amongst seven children—three brothers and four sisters. He was the youngest of the three brothers.

Young Piru was sent to the village school at the age of six or seven years. He did not like the restrictive environment of the school. One day, after a few months, he quarrelled with one of his classmates and when scolded by his class teacher he threw his slate at him and ran away from school never to go back. He helped his parents in the farm and grew into a strong, handsome and robust youth. He was fond of sports and games and of outdoor life and was often seen advising young men much older than himself. He was fond of shikar and despite an accident that caused serious injury to his chin, shikar continued to be his favourite sport.

From the beginning he was determined to join the Army. He was turned down twice because he was too young and was finally accepted at the age of eighteen. On 20 May 1936, Piru joined the Army and was posted to 10/1st Punjab at Jhelum. After a year's training he was posted to 5/1st Punjab on 1 May 1937.

Despite his earlier antipathy to school, Piru Singh took education in the Army seriously and within a few years passed the Indian Army First Class Certificate of Education and other tests and was promoted Lance Naik on 7 August 1940. During his tenure with this battalion he saw action on the North West Frontier.

In September 1941 he was posted as an instructor at the Punjab Regimental Centre at Jhelum, promoted Naik in March 1941, and Havildar in February 1942. He was an excellent sportsman and represented his Regiment in hockey, basket ball and cross-country. He stayed on at the Centre as an instructor till October 1945 and was appointed Company Havildar Major in May 1945. After the end of World War II he went to Japan in April 1946 to serve with the Commonwealth Occupation Forces and stayed there till September 1947.

By this time the country had been partitioned and the Rajput elements of 5/1st Punjab Regiment were transferred to the 6th Battalion of the Rajputana Rifles.

On the outbreak of hostilities in Jammu and Kashmir, Piru Singh was flown into the Valley with his battalion which played a very significant role in pushing the raiders back beyond Uri. In the summer offensive of 1948, Piru Singh displayed excellent qualities of leadership and courage during the operation for the capture of Pirkanthi and Ledigali.

His final example of leadership and cold courage was shown in the battle of Darapari where he lost his life and was awarded the nation's highest award for courage of the highest order in the face of the enemy.

Lance Naik Karam Singh, MM

1 SIKH

Operations in Tithwal and the Battle of Richmar Gali

Tithwal in Jammu and Kashmir was captured on 23 May 1948. After that date, the enemy made numerous attempts to recapture Richmar Gali and thereafter Tithwal. On 13 October 1948, coinciding with Id, the enemy decided to launch a brigade attack to retake Richmar Gali and then bypassing Tithwal to advance into the Srinagar Valley. 1 Sikh in Richmar Gali had to bear the burnt of the enemy attacks.

Using a brigade, the enemy made a series of vicious attacks in a supreme effort to drive out our troops from this area of vital importance. Under cover of heavy artillery and mortar fire the enemy put in a battalion attack on 1 Sikh positions which was repulsed after a stiff struggle at 0600 hours on 13 October. The enemy brought up more artillery, mortars and machine-guns and at 0930 hours the same day, another enemy battalion attacked. At 1000 hours the enemy attacked the main company position. This was repulsed with heavy casualties to the enemy. The enemy attacked again after bringing heavy and accurate artillery and mortar fire on the company-defended locality of 1 Sikh. This attack was also repulsed but by this time most of the bunkers of 1 Sikh had been destroyed. The air force was called in and managed to engage the enemy effectively. The company was reinforced by the Battalion Recce Group and two Companies of 3 Jat which with effective artillery support helped 1 Sikh to beat back the enemy. By this time the casualties suffered by 1 Sikh were 47—10 killed and 37 wounded.

The enemy made yet another serious attempt to dislodge our troops from Richmar Gali. After heavy mortar firing throughout the night of 13/14 October two enemy Companies launched an attack at 0730 hours on 14 October but were driven back with heavy losses. Our aircraft were also to effectively engage the enemy artillery and although enemy guns again opened heavy fire on our positions no further attack took place. The enemy's repeated attempts to take Richmar Gali finally failed.

Battle of Richmar Gali

It was in this fiercely contested action in the area of Richmar Gali in the Tithwal Sector that Lance Naik Karam Singh, MM, of 1 Sikh proved himself to be a dauntless leader of men in a critical situation.

On 13 October 1948 when the enemy in considerable strength attacked the 1 Sikh positions, Lance Naik Karam Singh, MM was commanding an outpost which was the enemy's first objective. Although it was attacked by vastly superior numbers, Lance Naik Karam Singh held on to his post manned by only four men, till ammunition ran low and two of the four were wounded. At this stage, fully aware that due to heavy shelling and continuous firing no help could be expected, Lance Naik Karam Singh although being wounded himself brought back his two wounded companions with the help of the third soldier and joined the main company defended locality.

In this forward company position, which was subject to heavy enemy shelling and fierce attacks, Lance Naik Karam Singh was again conspicuous by his gallantry. Though twice wounded he refused to be evacuated. By this time all the bunkers of his platoon had been destroyed but Lance Naik Karam Singh continued fighting and encouraging his comrades from the front-line trenches. The fifth enemy attack was very severe; two of the enemy came so close to Lance Naik Karam Singh's position that he jumped out of his trench, bayonetted the two attackers and jumped back into his trench.

The enemy attacked twice more but these too were beaten back. The enemy attack was finally called off at approximately 1900 hours. They had launched eight fierce attacks which were rendered unsuccessful due to the determination and courage of Lance Naik Karam Singh and his men. Throughout the battle, Karam Singh set a unique example of courage and devotion to duty. Lance Naik Karam Singh, MM was awarded the Param Vir Chakra for his outstanding courage in the face of the enemy. His devotion to duty and his leadership qualities constitute a unique example for all men to follow. Best of all, he lived to tell the tale.

* * *

Citation

Lance Naik Karam Singh
1 SIKH (NO. 22356)

Tithwal in Jammu and Kashmir was captured on 23 May 1948. After that date, the enemy made numerous attempts to recapture Richmar Gali, and thence Tithwal. On 13 October 1948, coinciding with Id, the enemy decided to launch a brigade attack to retake Richmar Gali and bypassing Tithwal, advance into the Srinagar Valley. Lance Naik Karam Singh was commanding a section at Richmar Gali.

The enemy commenced its attack with heavy shelling of guns and mortars. The fire was so accurate that not a single bunker in the platoon locality was left unscathed.

Communication trenches caved in. Bravely, Lance Naik Karam Singh went from bunker to bunker, giving succour to the wounded and urging the men to fight.

The enemy launched eight separate attacks that day. In one such attack, the enemy managed to obtain a foothold in the platoon locality. Immediately, Lance Naik Karam Singh, who was severely wounded by then, with a few men, hurled himself in a counter-attack and evicted the enemy after a close quarter encounter which accounted for many enemy dead, having been despatched by the bayonet.

Lance Naik Karam Singh proved himself to be a dauntless leader of men in crisis. Nothing could subdue him and no amount of fire or hardship could break his spirit.

His gallant actions on that day inspired his colleagues to face the massive onslaught unflinchingly. It was his fiercely proud spirit which was largely responsible for the gallant stand at Tithwal that day.

Gazette of India Notification
No. 2—Press/50

* * *

The Bold and the Brave

Courage has never been known to be a matter of muscle, it is a matter of the heart . . .

– Mahatma Gandhi

Karam Singh was born during World War I on 15 September 1915 and was brought up at village Sehna near Sangrur. His father Sardar Uttam Singh was a prosperous farmer and Karam could have continued in his footsteps. He was however 'fired up' by the stories of heroism and bravery during World War I narrated by soldiers of the Sikh Regiment of his village. Karam, a balanced and mature youth decided that he too would like to be part of these stories and legends and on 15 September 1941 was enrolled in the Army in 1 Sikh. Two and half years later, he was already a hero. His conduct under fire and the bravery and courage displayed by him in the 'Battle of the Admn Box' during the Burma campaign of World War II, won for him the award of the Military Medal (MM). He was then only a Sepoy.

Already war decorated at a young age, he was an example to the soldiers of his battalion. Those who knew him say he was a man of honour. 'Doing the right thing and doing it right' appeared to be his maxim in life. However, he enjoyed his life in the Army, in his battalion and in his regiment. A good sportsman, he excelled in pole vault and the high jump. In 1948 he again had an opportunity to demonstrate his character and the love of his regiment. What is it that made him perform those superhuman feats of courage and bravery during the battle of Richmar Gali? Was it his basic qualities of character, of his sense of duty, of doing what was right or was it the spirit of his regiment that motivated him to do the impossible? We do not know and can only guess. Honorary Captain Karam Singh passed away peacefully at his village in 1995 at the age of 80 years but his story will live on in his village, his regiment, and in the Army.

Operations in the Jammu Sector
Naik Jadunath Singh

1 RAJPUT

Operations in Naushera and the Battle of Taindhar

Concurrently with the offensive by the raiders to capture Srinagar, Pakistan organised an advance by the raiders into the Jammu Province also on the same date i.e., 20 October 1947. The raiders attempted to capture several important towns from Poonch in the north, to Kathua in the south-east. They surrounded the towns of Poonch, Kotli, Mirpur, Jhangar, Naushera, Bhimber and Rajouri. They also carried out raids into Chhamb, Akhnoor, Ranbir-Singh-Pura, Samba and Kathua. Despite being vastly outnumbered, the State Force Garrisons held on to these important towns and awaited relief by the Indian Army.

The Defence Committee of the Cabinet directed Army Headquarters to clear the raiders from the state of Jammu and Kashmir. Major General Kalwant Singh who had assumed command of all the forces in Jammu and Kashmir, (designated as Jammu and Kashmir Division), in turn issued orders on 16 November, part of which related to 50 Para Brigade. This brigade was given a number of tasks, two of which were to secure Naushera by 16 November, and establish a firm base at Jhangar by 17 November 1947. Meanwhile 50 Para Brigade located at Gurdaspur had already begun moving by road to Jammu and Kashmir. They would take a long time to reach because the road beyond Pathankot was in very poor condition.

Link-up with Poonch

Poonch was a strategically important town. Its loss would have provided Pakistan easy access to the Kashmir Valley without their forces having to advance on the obvious Domel-Srinagar route. It was planned that a link-up should take place with Poonch as early as possible. For this purpose, it was decided that relief columns would be sent both from Jammu in the south and Uri in the north. 50 Para Brigade was to advance via Naushera, Jhangar and Kotli to Poonch. The brigade commenced its advance on 13 November 1947. It reached Akhnoor the same day and Naushera and Jhangar on 18 November and on 19 November linked up with garrisons there. It fought its way to Kotli and linked up with the garrison there on 26 November. It was found that enemy resistance was stiffening, our troops inadequate, and the line of communication getting too long. The link-up with Poonch by this brigade was given up at this stage and it was ordered to return to Jhangar and to consolidate its position upto the area Jhangar-Naushera. Meanwhile there was a change of command of the Brigade and Brigadier Mohammad Usman took over on 7 December 1947.

Battle for Naushera

The enemy unhappy with the success of the Indian Army, started attacking its far-flung garrisons to restore confidence in its forces. It attacked Jhangar with 6000 raiders on the night of December 23/24 and succeeded in evicting a depleted battalion—2 Punjab.

By this time, it was apparent that the enemy's next objective would be Naushera itself. Brigadier Usman realised that he would have to take every possible measure to ensure its security. A hill feature named Kot, just to the north of Naushera was held by the enemy and completely overlooked Naushera town. It was necessary for the security of Naushera that this feature be captured at the earliest.

On 1 February 1948, 50 Para Brigade launched an attack at night and captured Naushera by the morning of 2 February. The enemy suffered heavy casualties and withdrew from the position. Enraged at this reverse, Pakistan launched a massive attack from different directions on 6 February with 15,000 raiders to recapture Naushera, and a grim battle ensued. Taindhar, a hill feature immediately overlooking Naushera received particular attention where repeated attacks were launched by the enemy. However, a battalion of Rajputs (1 Rajput) held on to this feature and inflicted very heavy casualties on the enemy. It was here that several gallant actions took place including hard hand-to-hand fighting, and it was here that many personnel received gallantry awards including the Param Vir Chakra (posthumous) awarded to Naik Jadunath Singh of the Rajput Regiment for valour of the highest order.

The Battle at Taindhar

Stung and mortified at the loss of Kot, the enemy launched an all-out attack on Naushera. The picquet at Taindhar received the brunt of the attack by 3000 Pathans of Swat and Dir, using mortars, machine-guns and grenades. The enemy, under cover of darkness had crept upto the Indian picquets and defensive locations on commanding features. At first light, the men in the picquets and posts saw thousands of armed men creeping up on them. In spite of heavy casualties, they came in wave after wave and hurled themselves at the picquets. The post at Taindhar halted three attacks on their barbed wire. By now, of the total of 27 men at the post, 24 were dead or wounded. Naik Jadunath Singh of 1 Rajput who was a Section Commander at this picquet, despite being wounded, displayed tremendous leadership and rallied and motivated his men, beating back each attack till he fell mortally wounded. His gallantry and supreme sacrifice earned him the Param Vir Chakra. His example inspired the surviving three men to continue defending their post. In hand-to-hand fighting, two were fatally wounded. The last man continued to defy the enemy. This was the critical moment of the battle for Naushera. Brigadier Usman, realising the gravity of the situation, had already sent a company of 3 (Para) Rajput to reinforce Taindhar, which reached just in time to prevent the enemy from overrunning this post. It was the turning point of the whole battle. If the company had not reached there in time, the Taindhar picquets would have been overrun and Naushera would have become untenable.

* * *

Citation

Naik Jadunath Singh
1 RAJPUT (NO. 27373)

At No. 2 picquet on Taindhar on 6 February 1948, No. 27373 Naik Jadunath Singh was in command of a forward section post which bore the full brunt of the enemy attack. The little post was garrisoned by nine men against overwhelming odds. The enemy launched its attack in successive waves and with great ferocity to overcome this post. The first wave swept up to the post in a furious attack. Displaying great valour and superb qualities of leadership Naik Jadunath Singh so used the small force at his disposal that the enemy retired in utter confusion. Four of his men were wounded but Naik Jadunath Singh again showed his qualities of good leadership by reorganising the battered force under him, for meeting another onslaught. His coolness and courage were of such an order that the men rallied and were ready for the second attack which came with greater determination and in larger number than the preceding one. Though hopelessly outnumbered, this post under the gallant leadership of Naik Jadunath Singh resisted. All were wounded, and Naik Jadunath Singh, though wounded in the right arm, personally took over the Bren gun from the wounded Bren gunner. The enemy was right on the walls of the post but Naik Jadunath Singh once again showed outstanding ability and valour of the highest order in action. By his complete disregard for his personal safety and example of coolness and courage, he encouraged his men to fight. His fire was so devastating, that what looked like impending defeat was turned into a victory and the enemy retreated in chaos leaving the dead and wounded littered on the ground. With this act of supreme heroism and outstanding example of leadership and determination, Naik Jadunath Singh saved the post from the second assault. By this time, all men in the post were casualties. The enemy put in his third and final attack in undiminished numbers and determination to capture this post. Naik Jadunath Singh, now wounded, prepared literally single-handed to give battle for the third time. With great courage and determination, he came out of the sangar and finally with the Sten gun, made a most magnificent single-handed charge on the advancing enemy, who, completely taken by surprise, fled in disorder. Naik Jadunath Singh, however, met his gallant death in his third and last charge when two bullets hit him in the head and chest. Thus, charging single-handedly at the advancing enemy, this Non-Commissioned Officer, performed the highest act of gallantry and self-sacrifice and by so doing saved his section—nay, his whole picquet from being overrun by the enemy at the most critical stage in the battle for the defence of Naushera.

Gazette of India Notification
No. 16—Press/50

* * *

Hanuman Bhagat Bal Brahmachari

Soldier, rest! thy warfare o'er
Dream of fighting fields no more;
Sleep the sleep that knows not breaking
Morn of toil, nor night of waking.

– Sir Walter Scott

Jadunath Singh was the third son of Birbal Singh Rathore and Jamuna Kanwar. Birbal Singh was a poor farmer in a remote village, Khajuri, in the Shahjahanpur district of Uttar Pradesh. Born in 1926, Jadunath was one of eight children— seven brothers and one sister—and did not have the fortune of having a good education.

He studied till class 4 in the village school and spent much of his time in helping his family work on the farm. He was the champion of the village in wrestling. He showed strong character from a young age and was soon nicknamed 'Hanuman Bhagat Bal Bramachari'. True to his name he never married.

He enrolled in the Rajput Regiment on 21 November 1941 at the Regimental Centre, Fategarh. After completing his training he was assigned to the 1st Battalion of the Rajput Regiment (now 4 Guards). He took part in World War II and showed glimpses of leadership and gallantry even at that time and was promoted to the rank of Naik and appointed Section

Commander. In this appointment he showed courage and determination of the highest order at the battle of Taindhar. His performance is a source of inspiration for others for all time to come.

Second Lieutenant Rama Raghoba Rane
BOMBAY ENGINEERS

The Recapture Of Rajauri

After the capture of Naushera and its valiant defence against the massive Pakistan counter-attack it was decided that the Indian forces should go on the offensive. The first task was the recapture of Jhangar which was achieved on 18 March 1948 by 50 Para Brigade and 19 Infantry Brigade.

It was now decided to maintain pressure on the enemy and to advance and capture Rajauri. The enemy held a number of defilés along the axis of advance, carried out extensive demolitions and erected numerous roadblocks. The advance involved the capture of Barwali Ridge, Chingas, and Rajauri in three successive phases. The advance commenced on 8 April, and the ridge was captured the same evening. The enemy counter-attacked but this was beaten back. The advance thereafter took place along the hills on either side of the road. Chingas was captured by the morning of 10 April. It was during this advance that a young Engineer Officer, Lieutenant Rane, cleared extensive mines along the axis at grave risk to himself to enable the armoured column to move on.

Second Lieutenant Rane was in charge of a mine-clearing party to clear the road to allow the column to advance. Although two of his party were killed and five including himself were wounded during these mine-and roadblock-clearing operations, he carried out his task fearlessly under incessant enemy fire. His superhuman efforts despite being wounded, cool courage, exemplary leadership and complete disregard for personal safety enabled the Indian tanks to reach Chingas. He was awarded the Param Vir Chakra for most conspicuous gallantry in the face of the enemy.

* * *

Citation

Second Lieutenant Rama Raghoba Rane
BOMBAY ENGINEERS (SS-14246)

On 8 April 1948, Second Lieutenant Rama Raghoba Rane, Bombay Engineers, was ordered to be in charge of the mine and roadblock clearing party at Mile 26 on the Naushera-Rajouri road which passes through very hilly country.

At 1100 hours, on that date near Nadpur South, just as Second Lieutenant Rane and his party were waiting near the tanks to start the work of clearing the mines ahead, the enemy started heavy mortaring of the area, with the result that two men of the mine-clearing party were killed and five others including Second Lieutenant Rane were wounded. The officer at once reorganised his party and started work for the tanks to go on to their position. Throughout the day he was near the tanks under heavy enemy machine-gun and mortar fire.

After the capture of Barwali Ridge at about 1630 hours, although knowing that the enemy had not been completely cleared of the area, Second Lieutenant Rane took his party ahead and started making a diversion for the tanks to proceed. He worked on till 2200 hours that night in full view of the enemy and under heavy machine-gun fire.

On 9 April he again started work at 0600 hours and worked on till 1500 hours when the diversion was ready for the tanks to proceed. As the armoured column advanced, he got into the leading carrier and proceeded ahead. After proceeding about half a mile he came across a roadblock made of pine trees. He at once dismounted and blasted the trees away. The advance continued. Another 300 yards and the same story was repeated. By this time it was getting on to 1700 hours. The road was curving round the hill like a snake. The next roadblock was a demolished culvert. Second Lieutenant Rane again got on with the job. Before he could start work, the enemy opened up with their machine-guns, but with super courage and leadership he made a diversion and the column proceeded ahead. The roadblocks were becoming numerous but he blasted his way through. It was now 1815 hours, and light was fading fast. The carrier came across a formidable roadblock of five big pine trees surrounded by mines and covered by machine-gun fire. He started removing the mines and was determined to clear the roadblock but the armoured column commander appreciating the situation got the column into a harbour area.

On 10 April 1948 at 0445 hours, Second Lieutenant Rane again started work on the roadblock in spite of machine-gun fire with the support of one troop of tanks. With sheer will power he cleared this roadblock by 0630 hours. The next thousand yards was a mass of roadblocks and blasted embankments. That was not all. The enemy had the whole area covered with machine-gun fire but with superhuman efforts, in spite of having been wounded, with cool courage and exemplary leadership and complete disregard for personal life, he cleared the road by 1030 hours.

The armoured column proceeded ahead and got off the road into the river bed of the Tawi but Second Lieutenant Rane continued clearing the road for the administrative column. The tanks reached Chingas by 1400 hours. Second Lieutenant Rane appreciating that the opening of the road was most vital, continued working without rest or food till 2100 hours that night.

On 11 April 1948, he again started work at 0600 hours and opened the road to Chingas by 1100 hours. He worked on that night till 2200 hours clearing the road ahead.

Gazette of India Notification
No. 5—Press/50

* * *

The Life and Times of Rama Raghoba Rane

Nothing great will ever be achieved without great men and men are great only if they are determined to be so.

– Charles de Gaulle

The Ranes are a martial race. They originally belonged to that clan of the Rajput Ranas which migrated to the south in search of new territories and founded small principalities. One group noted for its courage and spirit, settled down in Goa. It took the Portuguese fifty years to overcome the resistance put up by the Ranes. This was followed by a large scale exodus of this clan from Goa to adjoining Indian territory. One of that clan was the ancestor of Second Lieutenant Rane. He settled in Chendia, a tiny village in the North Kanara district of Mumbai.

Rama was the son of a police constable. He was born at Haveli in Dharwar district on 26 June 1918. He received his early education in district schools but it was haphazard due to his father's frequent transfers. The non-cooperation movement which started in 1930 influenced him profoundly. This alarmed his father and he moved his family to his native village at Chendia.

In 1940 World War II was in full swing. Raghoba now a youth of twenty-two decided to join the Army to satisfy his thirst for adventure and enrolled himself in the Bombay Engineers on 10 July 1940. Rane's exuberance and enthusiasm proved him to be easily the best in his batch and he was selected the 'Best Recruit', awarded the Commandant's cane and promoted to Naik.

After his training, he joined 28 Field Company which, with 26 Infantry Division, was fighting the Japanese in Burma. During the retreat from Burma, Rane with two sections was hand-picked to stay behind at Buthidaung to destroy ammunition dumps and a large number of vehicles. He and his team were able to do this in the face of the advancing Japanese. Their planned pick-up by the Navy did not materialise and they had to return to their lines by crossing a river that was being actively patrolled by the Japanese. Rane, however, was able to elude the Japanese and get his sections safely across the river and they joined the Division at Bahri Bazar. For his courage and tenacity he was immediately promoted Havildar.

His excellent character and leadership qualities marked him for selection for a commission as a Second Lieutenant prior to the Jammu and Kashmir Operations. His extraordinary performance in the operations of Jammu and Kashmir under enemy fire, his relentless determination and cold courage under sustained conditions of danger and his extraordinary valour beyond the call of duty won for him the nation's highest award for bravery—the Param Vir Chakra.

The 1948 Jammu and Kashmir operations were Rane's most glorious period in uniform and he retired as a Major on 25

June 1958. He, however, continued to serve as a re-employed officer and finally left the service on 7 April 1971. He passed away peacefully at Command Hospital Pune on 11 July 1994 after a brief illness. He is survived by his wife, three sons and a daughter.

Bhagat and Rane, VC and PVC, Legend and Legacy

Was it a matter of chance that two officers of the same corps and the same group of Engineers won the highest awards for cold courage under fire in almost similar circumstances?

Is the similarity of their respective acts of gallantry in different wars, on different continents, and at different times a coincidence or is it that one was so inspired by the other that he walked in his footsteps with his own lamp of courage lighting the way for the continuance of a tradition set by his illustrious predecessor?

Premindra Singh Bhagat won the Victoria Cross, the highest award for gallantry in the face of the enemy in the British Empire during World War II in the Middle East in 1941. Rama Raghoba Rane won the Param Vir Chakra, the highest award for gallantry in the face of the enemy in India during the Indo-Pakistan War of 1947–48 in Jammu and Kashmir.

Whatever the differences, the similarities are too striking and singular to ignore:

- Both officers were Second Lieutenants when they won their awards, and both were from the Bombay Engineers.
- The teams of both officers suffered severe casualties in terms of dead and wounded in the execution of their tasks.
- Both officers were honoured with their awards for courage in the face of gravest danger when clearing mines and roadblocks under enemy fire over a protracted period of time.
- Both officers survived to complete their respective missions which were similar i.e., the removal of mines and obstacles to allow armoured and administrative columns to move.
- The period of their acts of courage under fire was identical—96 hours.

Courage is a moral quality; it is not a chance gift of nature like an aptitude for games. It is a cold choice between two alternatives, the fixed resolve not to quit; an act of renunciation which must be made not once but many times by the power of the will. Courage is will power. 'Anatomy of courage'; Lord Moran, Book World.

* * *

Citation

Second Lieutenant P.S. Bhagat for the Victoria Cross

10 June 1941

His Majesty the King has been graciously pleased to approve of the award of the Victoria Cross to the undermentioned officer:

Second Lieutenant Premindra Singh Bhagat, Corps of Indian Engineers (serving with Royal Bombay Sappers and Miners).

For the most conspicuous gallantry on active service in the Middle East. During the pursuit of the enemy following the capture of Metemma on the night of 31 January/1 February 1941 Second Lieutenant Bhagat was in command of a section of a Field Company, Sappers and Miners, detailed to accompany the leading mobile troops (Bren Carriers) to clear the road and adjacent areas of mines. For a period of four days and over a distance of 55 miles this officer in the leading carrier led the column. He detected and supervised the clearing of fifteen minefields. Speed being essential, he worked at high pressure from dawn to dusk each day. On two occasions when his carrier was blown up with casualties to others and on the third occasion when ambushed and under close enemy fire, he himself carried straight on with his task. He refused relief when worn out with strain and fatigue and with an eardrum punctured by an explosion, on the ground that he was not better qualified to continue his task to the end.

His coolness, persistence over a period of 96 hours and gallantry, not only in battle, but throughout the long period when the safety of the column and the speed at which it could advance were dependent on his personal efforts, were of the highest order.

Authority: GHQ letter no. 66805/
E.I.B dated 17 September 1941

Conclusion of Operations in Jammu and Kashmir

The operations described are only those that were closely linked with the battles where our icons of courage won their awards. It would be inappropriate to conclude the narrative here without bringing the war to its conclusion, in order to inform the readers about what eventually happened.

The original plan of the Indian Army for the capture of Muzaffarabad could not be implemented due to inadequate troops and resources. Pushing beyond available operational and administrative capability would have been unreasonable. While the operations for the capture of Muzaffarabad were going on, Pakistan posed a fresh threat to Srinagar through a place called Gurais immediately to the north of Srinagar. The enemy was, however, also threatening Ladakh. General Thimayya sent a column to deal with this threat, captured Gurais by 27 June 1948 and pushed the enemy to the northern bank of the Kishanganga river.

Gilgit Agency which is a part of the northern region of Jammu and Kashmir was in the meantime lost due to a conspiracy hatched by Pakistan, aided and abetted by the British officers of the Gilgit Scouts, who raised the Pakistani flag over Gilgit. Skardu was also lost due to our inability to reinforce the garrison there. The raiders then moved down and captured Kargil and Dras, and infiltrated into Ladakh.

General Thimayya reacted quickly and flew in two Gorkha companies of 2/8 Gorkha Rifles into Leh and they arrived just in time to repulse two determined attacks by the raiders. As Zojila, Dras, and Kargil, on the road from Srinagar to Leh, were in enemy hands, the remainder of 2/8 Gorkha Rifles marched 320 kilometres to Leh through most difficult terrain and inhospitable weather conditions via Manali and Bara Lacha La and beat back several determined attacks by the enemy on Leh. With Ladakh now in safe hands, Zojila was attacked by 77 Para Brigade consisting of 1/5 Royal Gorkha Rifles (Frontier

Force), 5 Maratha, 1 Patiala, and 4 Rajput. Tanks of 7 Cavalry made history when they were used at these heights, to support the assaulting infantry. Despite heavy snowfall and blizzards the assault went in on 1 November 1948 and after some stiff fighting Zojila was cleared by the infantry. Armour was used beyond the pass and Dras was captured by 15 November. The enemy was now completely demoralised and Kargil was captured by 23 November. A link-up between 77 Infantry Brigade and the Leh garrison was effected on 24 November.

In the meantime, a United Nations Commission had arrived in India in early July 1948 and had appealed to both sides to stop all offensive operations. While India, as usual, responded to the appeal and stopped all offensive operations by her forces, Pakistan played a double game by accepting the appeal on the one hand and launching attacks on the other. It was as a result of her duplicity that Indian positions at Pandu, in the Uri Sector, and the hill feature north of the Kishanganga were lost. Although Pakistan had always maintained that she was not involved in the fighting in Jammu and Kashmir, she had to ultimately admit to the United Nations that her regular forces were fighting there. In this connection the following information that came to light is also relevant:

a) In an interview given to Brigadier A.R. Siddiqui, Major General Akbar Khan of Pakistan who commanded the Raiders under the pseudonym of 'General Tariq' stated, 'A few weeks after Partition, I was asked by Mian Iftikaruddin on behalf of Liaquat Ali Khan (Prime Minister of Pakistan) to prepare a plan of action for Kashmir . . . I was called to a meeting with Liaquat Ali Khan at Lahore where the plan was adopted, responsibilities allotted and orders issued.'

b) Major General (Retd) O.S. Kalkat, PVSM, in his book The Far Flung Frontiers has vividly brought out that while he was still in Pakistan on a staff assignment during Partition, he personally and by default, came across a highly classified document called 'Operation Gulmarg' which contained the Pakistani Plan for the invasion and capture of Jammu and Kashmir in 1947 and was signed by the then British Commander-in-Chief of the Pakistan Army.

The mustering of transport to convey the raiders from Peshawar to the border could also not have been made without the knowledge and participation of British civil officials.

Whereas a number of resolutions were passed in the UN aimed at restoring peace, Pakistan was never condemned by the West for its aggression. A UN Resolution of August 13, 1948 was finally accepted by both sides which envisioned the withdrawal of Pakistani troops from Jammu and Kashmir after which the will of the people would be decided by plebiscite. The ceasefire came into effect on 1 January 1949 but Pakistan never withdrew its forces. Although she never tires of blaming India for not holding a plebiscite, the prerequisite for withdrawing her forces is never mentioned by her. Her fatal obsession to capture Jammu and Kashmir by force has resulted in three more wars and her recourse to terrorism which continues till today.

CHAPTER II

THE
SINO–INDIAN WAR
1962

1962

Sino–Indian War

∎

If you don't run after your problems; your problems will run after you.

— Old Polish Proverb

A man cannot be too careful in the choice of his enemies.

— Oscar Wilde

The War in the East— NEFA

It has been said wars are caused by politicians, compounded by bureaucrats and fought by soldiers. The Sino-Indian War of 1962 was one such war where politicians failed the country in its hour of crisis. The route to the humiliating defeat of 1962 began soon after Independence when blinkered political vision allowed the nation's leaders to be seduced by the illusion of an alliance between Asia's two ancient civilisations. Unable to discern the duplicity of Chinese diplomacy, or to unravel the contradictions and incongruity of the Chinese mind, Prime Minister Jawaharlal Nehru continued to make unwarranted and ignominious concessions to an expansionist China. China's forceful occupation of peace-loving Tibet and India's abject response to China's aggression was symptomatic of China's expansionist tendencies and India's inability to stand up to what was morally, and blatantly wrong. Not only did India fail to condemn China's aggression but over a period of time continued to make humiliating excuses for her failure to do so. Worse, India's political

Pandit Jawahalral Nehru talking to Sikh troops somewhere in the North East Frontier Agency (NEFA), 1962.

leadership headed by Prime Minister Nehru, refused to upgrade the country's inadequate military machine. Unfortunately, a supine military hierarchy, after the departure of General Thimayya, allowed India's political bosses to further reduce its military effectiveness.

In addition to denying the Army the critical weapons and equipment it so badly needed, political interference in the promotion of senior Army officers had split its leadership. Using officers and men of the renowned 4th Indian Infantry Division to build houses instead of training for war reduced this famous Indian infantry division's military competence. It was this infantry division, that soon after the house-building episode, had to bear the brunt of the Chinese offensive in the East.

In short, the country failed to see the writing on the wall, and when the Chinese dragon turned its belligerent eyes on India, the nation's response was woefully wanting in direction, purpose and strength. Indian public opinion now took centre-stage and demanded that its vacillating and timorous leaders do something to salvage national pride and to get the Chinese to vacate Indian territory. The nation's demi-gods now realised too late the futility of their policy of prevarication. Unable to sustain public indignation and criticism, they now ordered an unprepared and ill-equipped army to 'throw the Chinese out'. An immature and irresponsible press went to town on these directions. The international press picked up these headlines and China got just the excuse she was waiting for. Fully anticipating such a situation, she had collected, trained, motivated and positioned her forces over a period of three years at strategic locations of her own choice.

The Indian Army was forced into a 'no-win' situation as a result of an incoherent politico-military strategy. Some of the Indian Army's finest units were placed in a situation where they were out-manned, out-gunned, and outmanoeuvred even before the war began. The result was a foregone conclusion and they were annihilated without a fighting chance.

'Victory' has many owners and 'Defeat' stands alone and unclaimed. Bravery and courage however recognise neither victory nor defeat. Amongst good soldiers, the greater the crisis, the greater the resolve to do one's duty, to carry out one's mission, and to do all that is necessary to protect the reputation and *izzat* (honour) of the nation. Fully aware of the disadvantageous position we were in, there were those who never faltered in the execution of their mission—even at the cost of their lives. Three such men's heroic actions in the Sino-India War of 1962 won for them India's highest award for courage in the face of the enemy.

This then is the story of three brave and gallant hearts who fought the Chinese army in the best way they could. Of the three, only one survived to tell the tale.

Subedar Joginder Singh

1 SIKH

The Battle at Bumla

On 8 September 1962, Prime Minister Nehru was in London for the Commonwealth Prime Minister's Conference. On 9 September, at a meeting held in India by the Defence Minister, Krishna Menon, a decision was taken to evict the Chinese south of the Thagla Ridge. Nehru was informed of the developments and he endorsed the decision. 7 Infantry Brigade was ordered to move to the Namka Chu—an area which was dominated by the enemy and tactically unsound. The Indian Press unfortunately blew up these developments with sensational headlines that projected a military offensive that our forces were incapable of implementing.

The Chinese, now fully aware of the confusion that prevailed in India, and the advantageous situation they were placed in, attacked the ill-prepared and tactically unsound Indian position at Namka Chu and overran it on 20 October 1962 with overwhelming strength. The Indian troops fought bravely but most of them died fighting with obsolete weapons, inadequate ammunition and a virtually non-existent line of communication.

Soon after the attack destroyed 7 Infantry Brigade at Namka Chu, the Chinese advanced towards Tawang. A divisional-sized force advanced across Bumla held by only a company of 1 Sikh. Hopelessly outnumbered, the company faced wave upon wave of Chinese soldiers. In the highest traditions of Indian chivalry, the brave soldiers of 1 Sikh led by Subedar Joginder

Singh faced the Chinese hordes with unwavering determination. Having decimated the initial Chinese assault, the platoon had sustained heavy casualties and was reduced to half its strength. Subedar Joginder Singh was wounded in the thigh but refused to be evacuated. When ammunition ran out, the remnants of this ragged platoon fixed bayonets, and unmindful of certain death, charged headlong into the advancing lines of Chinese attackers shouting the famous Sikh war cry *Bole So Nihal, Sat Sri Akal.* The Chinese assaulting lines wavered at the sight of these brave, bleeding, bearded warriors and many fell to the thrust of their flashing bayonets, but the overwhelming strength and superior weapons of the Chinese soldiers were able to absorb the last fearless charge of Subedar Joginder Singh and his gallant band of determined Sikhs. Most of them were killed or badly wounded. Subedar Joginder Singh was mortally wounded and died in Chinese captivity. Neither his body nor his remains were ever handed over.

* * *

Citation

Subedar Joginder Singh
1 SIKH (JC 1547)

Subedar Joginder Singh was the commander of a platoon of the Sikh Regiment holding a defensive position at a ridge near Tongpen La in NEFA. At 0530 hours on 23 October 1962, the Chinese opened a very heavy attack on the Bumla axis with the intention of breaking through to Towang. The leading battalion of the enemy attacked the ridge in three waves, each about 200 strong. Subedar Joginder Singh and his men mowed down the first wave, and the enemy was temporarily halted by the heavy losses it suffered. Within a few minutes, a second wave came over and was dealt with similarly. But the platoon had, by then, lost half its men.

Subedar Joginder Singh was wounded in the thigh but refused to be evacuated. Under his inspiring leadership the platoon stubbornly held its ground and would not withdraw.

Meanwhile the position was attacked for the third time. Subedar Joginder Singh himself manned a light machine-gun and shot down a number of the enemy. The Chinese however continued to advance despite heavy losses. When the situation became untenable Subedar Joginder Singh and the few men that were left in the position fixed bayonets and charged the advancing Chinese, bayonetting a number of them before he and his comrades were overpowered. Throughout this action, Subedar Joginder Singh displayed devotion to duty, inspiring leadership and bravery of the highest order.

Gazette of India Notification
No. 68—Press/62

* * *

Beyond Fear

Soldiers are citizens of death's grey land
Drawing no dividend from time's tomorrows.

– Unknown

Joginder Singh was born on 28 September 1921 and brought up at village Mahakalan near Moga in the Punjab. He did not come from a wealthy family and could not finish his studies in school due to financial reasons. He felt that the Army would give him a sense of identity and purpose, and was recruited into the Sikh Regiment. However, he was very keen on education and soon passed his Army education examinations and became a Unit Education Instructor. His drill and turnout were of an exceptional standard, as was his character.

He married in the early fifties and had a son and two daughters. A thoughtful and considerate person, he was loved and respected both at home and in his battalion. He did his duty to defend his country and the honour of his regiment to his last breath. His charge with the remnants of his platoon against the overwhelming hordes of Chinese attackers at Bumla is in keeping with his character and all that is characteristic of military chivalry and courage. In the face of overwhelming odds he pushed aside the fear of death and thoughts of his family. What was important to him was to defend India's frontiers at all cost. So, rallying his men, he led them in a last desperate attempt to rid his country of the invading enemy and perished in the attempt. His elder daughter died on hearing the news of her father's death. His son manages the land given to Joginder Singh's family by the Punjab government.

The War in the West— Ladakh

Ladakh, a part of the frontier province of Jammu and Kashmir, is also part of the Greater Himalayan Range. The mountains of

Ladakh, perhaps the most rugged and inhospitable in the world, are formidable. Leh, the capital, is at a height of approximately 10,000 feet and Chusul is at a height of 12,600 feet. The passes over which the roads had to be constructed were at heights ranging from 14,000 to 17,000 feet. The difficulties of operating and fighting at such heights can only be imagined.

On the Chinese side however the Tibetan Plateau is flat. The Chinese therefore could move in most areas even without roads. They had however constructed a motorable road from Gartok in Tibet to Sinkiang which sliced through the Aksai Chin taking away several hundred square kilometres of Indian territory. China's response to India's protests at its vast encroachments into its territory were vague and evasive with promises to solve the boundary question through mutual adjustment. India continued to be gullible. China, meanwhile, increased the number of her garrisons and built roads to ensure good communications.

Prime Minister Nehru had the benefit of a detailed letter from Sardar Vallabhbhai Patel twelve years before the war, outlining the threat from China (Annexure II) and advice from General Thimayya, the Indian Army Chief. He chose to ignore their advice. A defence plan made by General Thorat for the defence of Ladakh and NEFA was also rejected by the government. The Prime Minister instead chose to accept the advice of Mr Malik of the Intelligence Bureau, who as a civilian, recommended a plan for the Army called the 'Forward Policy' which entailed the setting up of a number of small posts facing the posts established by the Chinese.

Meanwhile, to counter the mounting criticism from the public against the Chinese incursions and our policy of appeasement, Pandit Nehru now decided to implement the Forward Policy against Army advice. His reasoning, based probably on Mr Malik's advice, that whoever established a post could establish a claim to that territory as the Chinese had done, was countered by the Army which argued that such posts were militarily unsound and unmaintainable and would be made untenable by Chinese superior forces. This was rejected by Pandit Nehru who, based on the advice given to him by a civilian, unqualified in defence matters, felt certain that whatever happened, China would never attack India.

As we have already seen, China launched her attack against our troops in the Eastern Sector on the night of 19/20 October 1962. On the same night she unleashed her forces against our troops in the Chip Chap, Galwan, and Pangong areas of Ladakh. Despite the fact that these posts were isolated, lacked fire support or any type of backing, they fought bravely but were overrun by the superior strength of the Chinese.

On 21 October 1962 the Chinese switched their offensive to the north of Lake Pangong. Their main objectives were Sirijap and Yula.

1/8 Gorkha Rifles who were at Sirijap fought it out to the end holding off the enemy long enough to allow the Yula post to withdraw in storm boats. Except for one who escaped, and two who were later known to have been captured, the Gorkhas all died fighting to the very last. The post commander Major Dhan Singh Thapa was awarded a posthumous Param Vir Chakra.

There was a lull in the fighting for nearly a month after which China once again resumed her offensive. On 17 November 1962, Chinese troops in considerable strength were seen moving for an attack on the Spangur Gap. 13 Kumaon was holding a feature south of the Spangur Gap that included Rezang La where a company of 13 Kumaon fought to the last under the courageous command of Major Shaitan Singh. Major Shaitan Singh was awarded the Param Vir Chakra for his outstanding courage. The award was posthumous.

It was later learnt that Major Dhan Singh Thapa was alive in Chinese captivity.

Major Dhan Singh Thapa
1/8 GORKHA RIFLES

The Battle at Sirijap

Sirijap 1 was a post established by 1/8 Gorkha Rifles on the northern bank of the Pangong Tso (Pangong Lake). Sirijap 1 was one of a series of posts established by the Indian Army as part of the Forward Policy in response to a large number of posts established by the Chinese in Ladakh. Between the months of September and November 1962, the Chinese and the Indians were jockeying for control of the area between the Pangong Tso and the Spangur Tso. The Chinese had the advantage of ground, greater numbers, and superior equipment.

'D' Company 1st Battalion the 8th Gorkha Rifles under the command of Major Dhan Singh Thapa had been given the task of preparing the post at Sirijap which dominated the surrounding area of approximately 48 square kilometres.

On account of the number of small posts that had to be established, only 28 men of 'D' company were available to hold Sirijap 1 and the Chinese quickly set up posts on three sides around it. Subedar Min Bahadur Gurung was the second-in-command.

On 19 October 1962, there was a dramatic increase in the strength of the Chinese forces around Sirijap with the arrival of a large body of troops with heavy weapons and guns. This was an indication that something was soon going to happen. There was a similar show of strength around the same time in the East, in the area of Thagla opposite Dhola. Anticipating an attack, Major Dhan Singh Thapa ordered his troops to 'dig fast and to dig deep'. This was easier said than done because the ground was very hard due to perma frost and the intense cold. The company commander ordered his men to use sand bags and ration bags to reinforce the defences as digging into such hard ground was not possible.

The expected attack by the Chinese commenced at 0430 hours on 20 October 1962 with a heavy concentration of artillery and mortar fire. This lasted for 2½ hours and provided the necessary cover to allow the Chinese to move upto 150 yards of the rear of the post. When the artillery fire lifted, they could hear the yells and screams of approximately 600 Chinese troops advancing to attack the post. This was the moment the Gorkhas were waiting for and when the assaulting troops came within range the Gorkhas went into action using their light machine-guns and rifles killing and wounding a large number of Chinese. The attack was broken up 100 yards from the post.

The artillery and mortar fire however had its effects on the troops of 'D' Company resulting in many killed and wounded. Naik Krishnabahadur Thapa, a Section Commander, although badly wounded took charge of one of the light machine-guns (LMG) after the crew had been killed. He continued firing the weapon till he himself was killed. The communication link with the battalion had in the meantime been destroyed.

The company commander Major Dhan Singh Thapa and his second-in-command Subedar Min Bahadur Gurung continued going from post to post making adjustments in the defences and encouraging the troops. Renewed artillery fire recommenced, more intense than the previous concentration and under cover of this fire the Chinese troops were able to crawl to within 50 yards of the Sirijap post. The enemy also commenced using incendiary bombs to set the post on fire and smoke out the defenders. The Gorkhas took up the challenge and using their hand-grenades and small-arms fire beat back this attack also. Subedar Min Bahadur Gurung was buried when his bunker collapsed on top of him. He was manning one of the LMGs at this time. He, however, dug himself out from the debris and recommenced firing the LMG causing heavy casualties amongst the Chinese till he himself was killed.

By now only seven of the 28 had survived and the post with Major Dhan Singh Thapa in command still held on. The enemy now brought in heavy machine-guns and bazookas and four amphibious craft on the lake each armed with two heavy machine-guns. Sirijap 1 continued to come under intense pressure. At this time, a small Indian storm boat made an attempt to link up the battalion headquarters from across the lake with Sirijap. This boat was manned by Naik Rabilal Thapa. He had been sent by the battalion headquarters to find out the fate of Sirijap 1 and had come from Tokung with another storm boat. Both boats were fired upon by the Chinese. One of the boats sank and all its occupants drowned. The second boat with Naik Rabilal Thapa in it managed to escape.

By this time, four of the surviving seven at Sirijap had also been killed and an incendiary bomb fell into Major Dhan Singh Thapa's bunker. He managed to extinguish the fire but by then the Chinese had overrun the post and Major Dhan Singh Thapa was overpowered and taken prisoner. The third attack by the Chinese was carried out with the use of tanks.

Naik Rabilal Thapa had, in the meanwhile, reported that Sirijap had fallen, that the post had fought till the end and that Major Dhan Singh Thapa and all the defenders had been killed. In actual fact three of the defenders had survived. Of these, Rifleman Tulsi Ram Thapa escaped and after four days of great adventure managed to elude the Chinese and joined the battalion. However it was much later that the battalion came to know that Major Dhan Singh Thapa had been taken prisoner by the Chinese.

* * *

Citation

Major Dhan Singh Thapa
1/8 GORKHA RIFLES (IC 7990)

Major Dhan Singh Thapa was in command of a forward post in Ladakh. On 20 October it was attacked by the Chinese in overwhelming strength after being subjected to intensive artillery and mortar bombardment. Under his gallant command, the greatly outnumbered post repulsed the attack, inflicting heavy casualties on the aggressors. The enemy attacked again in greater numbers after heavy shelling by artillery and mortar fire. Under the leadership of Major Thapa, his men repulsed this attack also with heavy losses to the enemy.

The Chinese attacked for the third time, now with tanks to support their infantry. The post had already suffered large numbers of casualties in the earlier two attacks. Though considerably reduced in number it held out to the last. When it was finally overrun by overwhelming numbers of the enemy, Major Thapa got out of his trench and killed several of the enemy in hand-to-hand fighting before he was finally overpowered by Chinese soldiers.

Major Thapa's cool courage, conspicuous fighting qualities and leadership were in the highest traditions of our Army.

Gazette of India Notification
No. 68—Press/62

* * *

Second Life

Courage is resistance to fear, mastery of fear, not absence of fear.

– Mark Twain

Major Dhan Singh Thapa was born on 10 April 1928 at Shimla, Himachal Pradesh and was commissioned into the 8th Gorkha Rifles on 28 August 1949. Like most Gorkhas, soldiering and its concomitants of duty, discipline, dedication, loyalty and integrity, came naturally to him. He was also an officer with a very cheerful disposition.

When as Officer Commanding, 'D' Company he was ordered to establish a post at Sirijap, he did so willingly, and cheerfully. He was neither the charismatic leader nor the aggressive warrior. He in fact was the type that did his duty quietly and efficiently without blowing his own trumpet or beating his own drum.

When Major Dhan Singh Thapa was ordered to strengthen the defences of Sirijap post against a Chinese attack he did so to the best of his ability with the resources that were available to him. He was fully aware of the dangers that loomed ahead and the risks involved. When the Chinese attacked, they attacked with unusual ferocity. They used machine-guns, artillery, rocket launchers, and tanks at this small gallant post manned by one officer, one Junior Commissioned Officer, and 28 men. Major Dhan Singh Thapa however was cool in the face of such ferocity. He went around his defences, strengthening breaches, replacing casualties, and encouraging his men. Three attacks were beaten back, but by then the defenders were reduced to three and the post completely destroyed and razed to the ground. Even at this stage, he did not give up and continued fighting till he was finally overpowered and captured. Major Dhan Singh Thapa's trials did not end here. After he was taken prisoner, he was treated very badly. Against all military convention he was made to undergo a series of punishments, firstly for causing so many casualties to their forces, and secondly because he refused to make statements against the government of India and the Indian Army. The Chinese at this time, were desperately trying to force soldiers from Nepal to make anti-Indian statements but though they tried very hard with Major Dhan Singh Thapa they failed miserably.

Major Dhan Singh Thapa was subsequently promoted to colonel's rank. After retirement he settled down at Lucknow and was appointed as a Director with Sahara Airlines. He passed away on 6 September 2005.

Major Shaitan Singh

13 KUMAON

The Battle of Rezang La

The battle of Rezang La will long be remembered in the annals of military history because of the incredible heroism displayed by a small group of Indian soldiers led by Major Shaitan Singh against overwhelming hordes of Chinese.

The enemy had tried to surprise the defenders of Rezang La by launching a silent attack but were discovered by a patrol from the Kumaoni Company. When the Chinese attack materialised, the Kumaonis were waiting for them with machine-guns on fixed lines and mortars on registered targets. As the Chinese came within range the Kumaonis opened up. The Chinese casualties were very heavy and with every weapon of the Kumaonis' firing, the gulllies in front of the three platoons were soon full of dead and wounded Chinese.

The surprise attack having failed, the Chinese began shelling Rezang La with mortars, RCL guns and rockets to blast the bunkers and sangars. No bunker in Rezang La could have survived such a heavy concentration of fire but there was never any thought of withdrawal.

After the forward platoons and the mortar position had been destroyed, the Chinese turned their attention to the company headquarters and the depth platoon. Major Shaitan Singh knowing he was surrounded, reorganised the company position. During this phase, he was hit by a burst of fire in one arm followed by a machine-gun burst in the abdomen.

When Rezang La was later revisited, dead jawans were found in the trenches still holding on to their weapons. Broken light machine-guns, and men holding on to the butts of rifles with the remaining portion blown off testify to the intensity of enemy fire. Every single man of this company was found dead in his trench with several bullet or splinter wounds. The two-inch mortar man died with a bomb still in his hand. The medical orderly had a syringe and a bandage in his hand when a Chinese bullet killed him. A dozen bodies of Ahirs were found outside their trenches indicating that they had in turn attacked the attacking Chinese when they were killed. Of the thousand mortar bombs with the defenders all but seven of them had been fired. These too were ready to be fired when the section was overrun.

By any test, every man of 'C' Company 13 Kumaon who fought and died at Rezang La was a hero. A grateful nation will remember them as such, and the name of Major Shaitan Singh who fired these men to fight to the last, will live forever in the pages of Indian history. The nation's highest decoration for gallantry, the Param Vir Chakra, was awarded to Major Shaitan Singh posthumously; and when his body was recovered, it was flown to his home town Jodhpur where it was cremated with full military honours.

* * *

Citation

Major Shaitan Singh
13 KUMAON (IC 7990)

Major Shaitan Singh was commanding a company of an infantry battalion deployed at Rezang La in the Chusul Sector at a height of about 17,000 feet. The locality was isolated from the main defended sector and consisted of five platoon defended positions. On 18 November 1962, the Chinese forces subjected the company position to heavy artillery, mortar and small-arms fire and attacked it in overwhelming strength in several successive waves. Against heavy odds, our troops beat back successive waves of enemy attack. During the action, Major Shaitan Singh dominated the scene of operations and moved at great personal risk from one platoon post to another sustaining the morale of his hard-pressed platoon posts. While doing so he was seriously wounded but continued to encourage and lead his men, who, following his brave example fought gallantly and inflicted heavy casualties on the enemy. For every man lost to us, the enemy lost four or five. When Major Shaitan Singh fell disabled by wounds in his arms and abdomen, his men tried to evacuate him but they came under heavy machine-gun fire. Major Shaitan Singh then ordered his men to leave him to his fate in order to save their lives.

Major Shaitan Singh's supreme courage, leadership and exemplary devotion to duty inspired his company to fight almost to the last man.

Gazette of India Notification
No. 68—Press/62

Valour Triumphs

When a man dies gloriously in war
Shall we not say that he is of the golden race.

– Unknown

Major Shaitan Singh was born at Jodhpur, Rajasthan, the son of Lieutenant Colonel Hem Singhji. From a young age, Shaitan Singh had decided to join the army. He was commissioned in the Kumaon Regiment on 1 August 1949.

During the 1962 Sino-Indian War, his battalion, 13 Kumaon, was deployed in the Chusul Sector. The Brigade Commander of this sector was also a Kumaoni, Brigadier T. N. Raina. 13 Kumaon was, at that time, the only all-Ahir battalion of the regiment.

13 Kumaon arrived in Jammu and Kashmir from Ambala in June 1962. They had never seen snow, and they were destined to fight the battle of their lives in one of the coldest and highest battlegrounds of the world. The Chinese troops in this sector were from the mountains of Sinkiang. The Chinese were equipped with modern weapons, whereas our troops were equipped with the .303 single-action Lee Enfield rifle which was an obsolete and outmoded weapon of World War II. Notwithstanding the disadvantages of climate, terrain, and weapons, Major Shaitan Singh and 'C' Company, 13 Kumaon went all out to make sure that their defensive position at Rezang La would make the enemy pay heavily if they attacked. Every approach was covered by automatic and mortar fire. The disadvantage of the Rezang La position however was that because of its high crestline it was difficult for our artillery to support it.

The Chinese suffered very heavy casualties during their successive attacks on Rezang La, and the gullies and ground around the defences of 'C' Company were filled with the bodies of Chinese soldiers. However, the preponderance of numbers and the superiority of their weapons tilted the balance in their favour. So heavy was the bombardment by the Chinese artillery and mortars of various calibre that the post at Rezang La was totally obliterated and all the defenders killed. Major Shaitan Singh was wounded first in the arm and subsequently by a machine-gun burst in his abdomen. His men tried to evacuate him, but realising that he would be an impediment to them, he ordered them to leave him where he was. Three months later, his body was found at the same spot.

The man who inspired the troops to fight to the last man and the last round was Major Shaitan Singh. Except for a very few, every man of 'C' Company, 13 Kumaon, died at his post, and all ammunition had been exhausted. Months later, the bodies of the defenders of Rezang La were found frozen at their posts, defiant in death to the very last. The body of Major Shaitan Singh was recovered and flown to Jodhpur, where it was cremated with honours befitting a national hero.

Conclusion of the Sino-Indian War

If I always appear prepared, it is because, before entering on an undertaking, I have thought about it for a long time and have foreseen what may occur. It is not genius which reveals to me suddenly and secretly what I should do in a crisis. It is deliberation and forethought.

– Napoleon

It was obvious from the manner in which the Indian Army had to fight the Chinese in NEFA and Ladakh in 1962 that a proper political appreciation of the Chinese threat had not been made. Prime Minister Nehru, ably supported by his Defence Minister Krishna Menon who took a whimsical view that China would never attack India. This, in the face of overwhelming evidence that this is exactly what the Chinese in fact were preparing to do. It is also tragic that our higher military commanders meekly acquiesced to faulty decisions on military strategy by their political bosses knowing fully well that they were wrong.

When the Chinese entered Indian territory in September 1962, the government was in a quandary. The Indian public by now had had enough and was indignant at the government's inept handling of the situation with China and was clamouring for action. The government had by now long lost the initiative in the game of 'push and shove'. It now suddenly decided in the face of the public clamour to show itself to be bold and decisive. Without waiting for a senior officer to reach the Namka Chu to assess the Chinese threat, the government took a decision to announce that it had given orders to the Army to evict the Chinese from Indian territory. A most charitable view of such an announcement is that the Prime Minister and the Defence Minister continued to persist in their weird belief that the Chinese would never launch a full-scale attack on India, and that their order was only a bluff that would mollify the Indian public. The Defence Minister pushed the Chief, the Chief pushed the Army Commander, and the Army Commander pushed the nearest Brigade Commander to the Namka Chu. The bluff may have worked with the Indian public but it failed to work on the Chinese. It in fact gave them just the excuse and the opportunity they were looking and waiting for and they launched full-scale attacks both in NEFA and Ladakh. The Indian Army without adequate arms, ammunition equipment and high-altitude clothing and located on indefensible ground fought valiantly with whatever means they had and were quickly vanquished. Many brave and famous regiments and formations had to stomach the ignominy of defeat for no fault of their own. According to Nirad C. Chaudhuri, 'The political authorities had asked the soldiers to open an offensive without giving them a chance to win. The contemplated offensive was never approached as a military measure. It was insisted upon in the most frivolous manner out of a sense of political expediency.' The government's decision has since been characterised as a plain act of political opportunism in the face of the clamour of the Opposition and the uninformed public. No nation should ever allow itself to fight a war for which it is not prepared. An army that is ignored and neglected and whose leadership is rendered redundant by political interference can never fight, leave aside win a war. The American magazine *Time* when reporting on the Sino-Indian war of 1962 said, 'The Indian Army needs almost everything except courage.'

And courage was very much in evidence wherever the troops were well led. Examples were available at Bumla, Jang, Sirijap and Rezang La where the Chinese suffered very heavy casualties. At these places and at Dhola the troops offered valiant resistance in the face of hopeless odds and inevitable disaster. After the ceasefire, the Kumaonis at Rezang La were all found frozen at their posts—dead to a man, broken weapons in their hands, all ammunition exhausted, with plenty of evidence all around of the carnage they had wrought on the attacking Chinese.

It was at Bumla, Sirijap and Rezang La that Subedar Joginder Singh, Major Dhan Singh Thapa and Major Shaitan Singh led their troops defiantly against impossible odds in the true spirit and tradition of the Indian Army. All three were awarded the Param Vir Chakra but only Major Dhan Singh Thapa lived to tell the tale.

CHAPTER III

THE
INDO-PAKISTAN WAR
1965

1965
Indo-Pakistan War

■

*Wars are won or lost in the mind, before they are won or lost on the
ground.*

– Brigadier Desmond Hayde, MVC

Pakistan's bid to Annexe Jammu and Kashmir for the Second Time

Pakistan's obsession to take Jammu and Kashmir by force tempted her early in 1965 to replicate her earlier attempt of 1947–48. India had suffered a severe reverse in the Sino-Indian War of 1962—her economy had suffered substantially, reorganisation of her forces was incomplete, arms-aid after the war with China was only for the mountains and that too had yet to be absorbed. Pandit Nehru had died and his replacement, the diminutive Lal Bahadur Shastri, did not seem to impress the Pakistanis. Pakistan felt that the opportunity was too good to be wasted and needed to be taken advantage of. Her own economy was sound due to agricultural production and industrial growth. Significant economic assistance and massive military aid had been received from the United States amounting to 1.5 billion dollars at that time. This included over 200 M-45 Patton tanks, one squadron F-104A Supersonic Star Fighters, four squadrons F-86 Fighters (Sabre jets) and two squadrons B-57 Bombers. This completely upset the relative strength between India and Pakistan. Pakistan had also substantially improved her relations with China. General Ayub Khan who had come to power in a military coup apparently felt that the opportunity was ripe to once again attempt to take Jammu and Kashmir by force.

Before embarking on her plan for the annexation of Jammu and Kashmir, Pakistan decided to take a measure of India by launching a limited offensive in the desert area of the Rann of Kutch. She felt that this would give her an opportunity to test the calibre of the armour, arms and equipment freshly acquired from the United States and to also ascertain the resolve and will of the government of India under the leadership of Lal Bahadur Shastri. Pakistan commenced her offensive in the Rann of Kutch by attacking Sardar Post, a border police post, on 9 April 1965 with a brigade and quickly overran it. India's reaction was predictably slow. She reinforced the area with some of her regular forces. Pakistan responded by launching a divisional-sized attack under Major General Tikka Khan, supported by her newly acquired Patton tanks. A spirited resistance by the outnumbered and outgunned Indian defenders failed to convince a belligerent Pakistan that there was any need to deviate from her predisposed aggressive agenda. On the contrary, she seemed to be convinced that she held all the cards of a winning hand and that success in Jammu and Kashmir was guaranteed.

Pakistan, however, agreed to a ceasefire and a restoration of the situation to *status quo ante* in accordance with an agreement signed on 30 June 1965 pending arbitration by a three-man tribunal.

The Ceasefire Agreement brokered by the British seemed to convince India that all was well. Alarm bells did not begin to ring even though by now India ought to have understood

Pakistan's legacy of disinformation and deceit. While agreeing to the ceasefire on one hand she began to engineer a series of violent incidents on the border with Jammu and Kashmir as a prelude to 'Operation Gibraltar'.

Between 5 and 10 August 1965 Indian troops in Kashmir discovered infiltration at a mass scale in columns of 100 or more all over Kashmir. The infiltrating columns managed to capture a few lightly held posts and to isolate a few others. Captured prisoners and documents revealed a deliberate plan by Pakistan to capture Kashmir by guerrilla assault and an expected uprising of the locals from within the state. A special force of over 30,000 guerrillas armed and trained in Pakistan had been organised for this purpose. Each company was commanded by an officer of the Pakistan Army and consisted of the regular army as well as irregulars. The Pakistanis code-named this offensive as *Operation Gibraltar*.

Pakistan as usual denied complicity and called it an 'uprising'. History was being rewritten! Clear evidence of Pakistan involvement was available and was reported as such by the UN Military observer and by the Secretary General U. Thant at the Security Council on 3 September 1965. Interrogation of Pakistani prisoners of war (POWs) revealed that plans for *Operation Gibraltar* were made in May 1965—a month before the Rann of Kutch Agreement. Further the President of Pakistan, General Ayub Khan had himself addressed the Force Commanders at Murree in the second week of July 1965. So much for trusting Pakistani promises!

The Pakistani strategy banked on a revolt being engineered by the guerrillas and a collapse of the state government after which Pakistani regular forces would attack. Pakistan felt that Indian Army defences would collapse after being sandwiched between assaults on their defences by the Pakistani regulars on one side and guerrilla forces and a civilian revolt on the other.

However, things don't always go according to plan. The guerrilla groups were either destroyed, dissipated or dispersed.

The expected revolt did not take place, and it was discovered that the infiltrators were from Pakistan and not Kashmiris as projected by her. India decided to eliminate the guerrilla bases from where these forces operated and Haji Pir and Pir Saheba were captured in daring operations.

Pakistan responded by an offensive across the International Border (IB) with a divisional-sized force supported by an armoured brigade and heavy artillery. Chhamb and Jaurian were captured and their offensive was stopped 6 km short of Akhnur. In keeping with past pretences, Pakistan once again denied the use of regulars and termed this offensive (Operation Grand Slam) by POK (Pakistan Occupied Kashmir) forces. Pakistani aircraft also attacked our installations in Amritsar.

India's patience was now pushed beyond the restraint that she has always maintained when dealing with Pakistan and she decided to launch operations across the IB in areas of her own choosing and to also prepare for the inevitable Pakistani riposte.

It is not my intention to go into the detailed operations in this sector. However, a brief description of the action where the two Param Vir Chakras were awarded is desirable.

In accordance with our plans to cross the border in areas of our choosing, the Indian Army's 11 Corps was given the task of securing the line of the Ichhogil Canal, establishing bridgeheads across the canal and posing a threat to Lahore. It was expected that Pakistani forces would react violently and provide 11 Corps an opportunity to destroy them. It was decided that Asal Uttar would be a suitable place to cover an enemy offensive rather than Khem Karan which could be bypassed. Asal Uttar covered both, the Khem Karan-Amritsar axis, as well as the Khem Karan-Patti axis. The Pakistani Armoured Brigade attacked exactly as anticipated on 10 September 1965 and attempted to break through the position. First, they tried to overrun the 4 Grenadiers' position. This battalion held out with great determination and gallantry against heavy pressure by the enemy. In this action Company

Quartermaster Havildar Abdul Hamid was awarded the Param Vir Chakra (posthumous) for destroying a number of Patton tanks with his RCL gun. Despite repeated attempts to break through the Indian defences at Asal Uttar, the Pakistanis were unable to make any headway and suffered tremendous losses. A total of 97 tanks were lost by Pakistan in this area. 32 tanks in good running condition were captured by our troops and the General Officer Commanding the Pakistan Armoured Division was wounded and his Commander Artillery Brigade was killed when they came forward to the area of 4 Grenadiers to investigate why their tanks were not moving forward. Having lost the ability to continue the offensive any further, the Pakistani Commander-in-Chief called off the offensive and pulled out the remnants of Pakistan's 1 Armoured Division to meet the threat of India's 1 Corps offensive in the north.

In the meanwhile India's 1 Corps, a newly raised formation, was given the task of isolating Sialkot from Lahore. The capture of Chawinda was part of this operation and it was here that Lieutenant Colonel A.B. Tarapore of Poona Horse (17 Horse) distinguished himself and was awarded the Param Vir Chakra (posthumous).

Company Quartermaster Havildar Abdul Hamid

4 GRENADIERS

The Battle of Asal Uttar, 1965, Version of 4 Grenadiers and the Grenadier Regimental Centre

4 Grenadiers is a unique example of a battalion that distinguished itself in an intensely fought war without its regular company commanders and specialist platoon commanders. They had gone to the Indo-Tibetan border as the 'Advance Party' in accordance with an earlier relief programme. Company officers and Junior Commissioned Officers were consequently elevated to fight this battle and Abdul Hamid who was the Company Quartermaster Havildar was directed to take over a detachment of RCL guns of his battalion. This was done to make best use of the four RCL guns issued to the battalion just before commencement of operations. No. 2639885 Company Quartermaster Havildar Abdul Hamid had done well on the RCL course at Infantry School, Mhow and that is how a Company Quartermaster Havildar came to be in charge of a detachment of RCL guns.

The battalion arrived at midnight from the area of the Ichhogil Canal and commenced frantically to dig down. By dawn of 8 September the trenches had gone down barely three feet. No overhead cover was possible and no camouflage necessary as the battalion was in the midst of thick sugarcane fields.

At 0730 hours on 8 September the rumbling of a large number of enemy tanks was heard. At 0900 hours a troop of Pattons came astride the road. The Grenadiers held their fire and when the leading tank was 30 yards away Company Quartermaster Havildar Abdul Hamid knocked it out. The crew of the two follow-up tanks abandoned their tanks and fled.

At 1130 hours came a second attack by two troops of enemy armour preceded by heavy artillery shelling. Abdul Hamid knocked out yet another tank, his second, and again the crew of two follow-up tanks abandoned their tanks and fled. At the end of the day Abdul Hamid had destroyed two enemy Patton tanks and four tanks had been abandoned.

In response to frantic demands for mines, an Engineer Company came forward and laid anti-tank and anti-personnel mines.

At 0900 hours on 9 September 1965, the Grenadier position was attacked by four Sabre jets without causing any casualties. The air attack was followed by three more armour assaults at 0930, 1130 and 1430 hours. Abdul Hamid destroyed two more tanks and some anti-tank mines were heard exploding. By the evening of 9 September Abdul Hamid had destroyed four Patton tanks. The battalion had accounted for 13 tanks and more lay abandoned in the minefield.

It was clear by now that the battalion was facing a concentrated assault by an armoured formation, possibly of brigade strength. A squadron of Shermans was withdrawn as their shells were ineffective against the armour of the Patton tanks.

The Centurion tanks which had come forward briefly were also withdrawn to an area more suitable for a tank battle. 4 Grenadiers was left to fight an armoured division with just its RCL guns, a hastily scattered minefield and the determination of its men. The morale of the men, however, was sky-high. After all, they had with their RCL guns destroyed more enemy tanks than an armoured formation could ever hope for in a tank-to-tank battle.

On 10 September the battalion defences were heavily shelled. A dawn attack by infantry supported by armour was expected. However, the assault pattern remained the same as on the previous two days. The first thrust came at 0830 hours by a troop of tanks—one tank on the road and two other on the lower verges of the road about 200 yards away. Strict fire discipline was observed and when the tanks came close enough. Abdul Hamid destroyed one more tank and moved his RCL gun to another fire position. At 0900 hours the enemy again pressed forward with increased artillery support and Abdul Hamid destroyed one more tank—his sixth. This was followed by heavy artillery shelling. Due to his open RCL jeep being vulnerable to shelling, Abdul Hamid moved his jeep to another firing position and told the rest of his crew to take cover.

The next tank and Abdul Hamid spotted each other simultaneously. Being alone, he could not change his position, so he reloaded his weapon and traversed it. The Pakistani tank gunner and Abdul Hamid placed each other in the cross-hairs of their sights together and fired almost simultaneously. Abdul Hamid was killed instantly. It is not clear whether the enemy tank was also destroyed. The battalion history however states that both fired simultaneously and blew each other to bits.

Abdul Hamid was awarded the Param Vir Chakra posthumously and the battalion the battle honour of Asal Uttar and the theatre honour 'Punjab'.

Not to be forgotten is the dramatic manner in which the General Officer Commanding of the Pakistani Armoured Division and his Commander Artillery found themselves within the forward defences of 4 Grenadiers. At about 1100 hours, the enemy General Officer Commanding came forward to see for himself why his leading tanks kept disappearing into the sugarcane and were out of communication. Some time earlier, three RCL jeeps had entered the battalion defences in this area. Two of these jeeps were destroyed by the boys in the forward trenches but the third jeep got away. These jawans got a dressing down for poor fire discipline and were told they were not to open fire without express orders from their Company Officer. So, when the enemy General Officer Commanding drove up, the men held their fire. One of them stood up. The General Officer Commanding, thinking him to be a Pakistani straggler, told him to come up to him. On the boy refusing to go up to him, the General Officer Commanding got down and this is when the two remaining men stood up and pointed their rifles at him. The General Officer Commanding reached for his pistol, and at this point, the men fired at the General Officer Commanding and his group. The General Officer Commanding, the Commander Artillery and the occupants of all the vehicles were reported as killed. The Rover managed to turn around and drive away. After a few minutes, a message on the enemy General Officer Commanding's Rover was intercepted. '*Bara Imam mara gaya (the chief is no more)*.' The General Officer Commanding's 'R' Group had also been escorted by armour. These tanks now formed a protective shield around the General Officer Commanding who was taken away. The battalion during this period was subjected to very heavy fire, and was short of RCL ammunition.

Full credit must be given to Lieutenant Colonel Farad Bhatti, his band of very junior officers and 4 Grenadiers for their excellent and courageous performance in helping to stem the thrust of the Pakistan Armoured Division Offensive which happened to come astride the 4 Grenadiers battalion defended the area.

Version of the Official History of the Army as Disclosed by The Times of India *and Downloaded from the Internet.*

Pakistan's attempt to overrun 4 Grenadiers during the early hours of 9 September 1965 had already failed. Pakistani forces carried out 'recce in force' with tanks throughout the latter part of 9–10 September 1965.

The final enemy attack came at 0645 hours on 10 September 1965. Pakistani tanks came in area Manwan with a view to bypassing the Indian defended sector. At 0830 hours, one enemy combat group from Pak 4 Armoured Brigade was launched against 4 Grenadiers but the attack was foiled by artillery concentrations before the enemy infantry could close in on to the Indian minefields. Indian armour then came from the flanks resulting in a tank mêlée. Here, an RCL gun manned by Company Quartermaster Havildar Abdul Hamid knocked out three Patton tanks and was posthumously awarded the first Param Vir Chakra in the division during the War. An outflanking move towards Mehmoodpura-Dibbipura by 4 Cavalry (Pak) Pattons was then noticed. Indian 3 Cavalry tanks hinging on the battalion-defended sector shadowed these enemy tanks, which were finally trapped in area Mehmoodpura.

It was at 1400 hours 10 September 1965 that General Officer Commanding (General Officer Commanding) Pak 1 Armoured Division, Major General Nasir Ahmed, who had earlier witnessed the battle from a helicopter came with his 'R' (Reconnaissance) Group to the area of Mile 37 on the road Khem Karan-Bikhiwind to push the advance personally. The party was surprised by 4 Grenadiers and heavy artillery concentrations and the entire 'R' Group was destroyed at about 1800 hours. After the death of the Pak General Officer Commanding, the destruction of two combat groups and the 'R' Group of 1 Armoured Division (Pakistan), the enemy offensive was effectively foiled. However it was confirmed only on the morning of 11 September 1965 that the enemy advance had been held when officers and men of 4 Cavalry started surrendering. Thus the enemy's drive with a superior force of armour of five Patton regiments i.e., 4 Cavalry, 5 Horse, 6 Lancers, 19 Lancers and 24 Cavalry and one Chaffee Regiment (12 Cavalry) which had been directed to capture all territory West of River Beas and to cut off Khemkaran was stopped. At approximately 1700 hours one squadron of Centurions came into the positions of 4 Grenadiers and fired

at the enemy. The enemy tanks meanwhile withdrew towards
Bhura Kunah.

On searching the area, it was found that the entire 'R' Group
of Pak 1 Armoured Division had been surprised and destroyed in
this encounter. The body of Brigadier A.R. Shammi Commander
Pak Artillery Brigade of Pak 1 Armoured Division and some
others were recovered and buried. The documents captured
revealed that the other officer killed whose body was recovered
by the Pak tanks was that of the General Officer Commanding
1 Armoured Division. His collar gorget patches were also found
lying on the spot.* The captured documents also revealed the
entire plan of Pak 1 Armoured Division, which envisaged a
quick advance and deep penetration into Indian territory upto
Harike Bridge, Beas and Amritsar. A diary belonging to Major
John Hamilton Gardner of 24 Cavalry of a Pakistani armoured
regiment was recovered from a knocked out tank. This diary
contained the orders issued to his regiment and confirmed the
ambitious plan of the enemy, which had been thwarted by 4
Grenadiers.

The badges of rank of the Pakistani Commander Artillery
Brigade, who was killed and the collar gorget patches of the
Pakistani General Officer Commanding 1 Armoured Division
can be seen in the War Museum of 4 Infantry Division.

---

* According to Pakistani sources, the General Officer Commanding Major General
  Nasir Ahmed was wounded, not killed and subsequently removed from command
  for poor performance of his division.

Citation

Company Quartermaster Havildar Abdul Hamid
4 GRENADIERS (NO. 2639985)

At 0800 hours on 10 September 1965 Pakistan forces launched an attack with a regiment of Patton tanks on a vital area ahead of village Cheema on the Bhikkiwind road in the Khem Karam Sector. The attack was preceded by intense artillery shelling. The enemy tanks penetrated the forward position by 0900 hours. Realising the grave situation, Company Quartermaster Havildar Abdul Hamid who was commander of a RCL gun detachment moved out to a flanking position with his gun mounted on a jeep, under intense enemy shelling and tank fire. Taking an advantageous position, he knocked out the leading enemy tank and then swiftly changing his position, he sent another tank up in flames. By this time the enemy tanks in the area spotted him and brought his jeep under concentrated machine-gun and high-explosive fire. Undeterred, Company Quartermaster Havildar Abdul Hamid kept on firing on yet another enemy tank with his recoiless gun. While doing so, he was mortally wounded by an enemy high explosive shell.

Havildar Abdul Hamid's brave action inspired his comrades to put up a gallant fight and to beat back the heavy tank assault by the enemy. His complete disregard for his personal safety during the operation and his sustained acts of bravery in the face of constant enemy fire were a shining example not only to his unit but to the whole division and were in the highest traditions of the Indian Army.

Gazette of India Notification
No. 111—Press/65

Tank Destroyer

*The difference between the impossible and the possible lies in
a man's determination.*

– T. Lasorda

Abdul Hamid was born on 1 July 1933 at village Dhamupur
in district Gazipur, in Uttar Pradesh. He belonged to 'C'
Company of 4 Grenadiers. 'C' Company was a Muslim
Company composed of 75 per cent Khaim Khani Muslims, the
remainder being Muslims from UP. Prior to the Indo-Pakistan
War of 1965 the Khaim Khani Muslims of 'C' Company were
needed to form the nucleus for the raising of additional
Khaim Khani Muslim Companies for the Grenadier Regiment
and the composition of 'C' Company 4 Grenadiers changed
to purely Muslims from UP. The reputation and honour
of the UP Muslims as fighting soldiers of the Grenadier
Regiment therefore fell upon the shoulders of the senior Non-
Commissioned Officers of 'C' Company.

4 Grenadiers at that time, formed part of 4 Mountain
Division. Being a mountain division, with a lesser tank threat,
the unit was not equipped with the anti-tank 106 RCL gun,
and therefore no training had been carried out in the unit for
the previous three years. Also, the advance party of the unit
with the officiating second-in-command, all company second-in
commands, and all specialist weapon detachment commanders
had moved to their new location. Fate however intervened.
Due to the Pakistani offensive in the Rann of Kutch in April
1965, the unit was ordered to move forward and to collect
its 106 RCL guns from the nearest Ordnance Depot. Prior to
this, the unit had the unique distinction of having five Non-
Commissioned Officer instructors at the same time at the
anti-tank wing of the Infantry School, Mhow. Some of these
instructors had reverted to the unit. Abdul Hamid was one of

them, and being one of the senior Non-Commissioned Officers, he was appointed Company Quartermaster Havildar. However, due to the absence of the anti-tank detachment commanders, he was told to take over an anti-tank detachment. That is how he, as a Company Quartermaster Havildar was handling an anti-tank detachment in war. These expert anti-tank gunners with their new anti-tank guns made all the difference to the outcome of this battle in the Khem Karan Sector. Abdul Hamid therefore, was the right man, at the right place, at the right time.

Although Abdul Hamid has been honoured with the nation's highest award for courage in the face of the enemy, it appears that his citation does not give him full credit for the number of tanks that he destroyed. Whereas the Regimental and Battalion Accounts give a detailed account of the seven tanks destroyed by him, it is not clear whether the seventh tank that destroyed him was itself destroyed by him, and as to why the citation gives him credit for only three tanks. After talking to officers who were serving in the unit at that time, and also the Commanding Officer, it transpires that the citation for Abdul Hamid's Param Vir Chakra was sent on the evening of 9 September 1965 after he had knocked out three enemy tanks. On 10 September 1965 he destroyed three more tanks and was killed when he had engaged the seventh enemy tank. When a follow-up message was sent informing the headquarters that Abdul Hamid was no more, the citation was amended to a posthumous award but it appears that the concerned persons failed to amend the total number of tanks destroyed by him to six or seven, as the case may be. The record needs to be set right.

Lieutenant Colonel A.B. Tarapore
POONA HORSE (17 HORSE)

The Battle of Chawinda

The capture of Chawinda was part of the overall design of 1 Corps in its operations in the Sialkot Sector. Poona Horse (17 Horse) commanded by Lieutenant Colonel A.B. Tarapore had a key role to play in this plan.

The area of Chawinda was held by about two regiments of Pakistan armour and infantry. 1 Armoured Brigade of which 17 Horse was a part launched its attack on 14 September 1965 but could secure only part of its objectives. Owing to heavy opposition encountered at Chawinda, the General Officer Commanding 1 Corps decided that unless a strong force was established behind Chawinda, and the position cut off, it would not be possible to capture the town. Thus 17 Horse and 8 Garhwal Rifles were ordered to establish themselves in the Jassoran-Butur-Dograndi area on 16 September. On the morning of 16 September 17 Horse with a company of 9 Dogra captured Jassoran after suffering heavy losses. 8 Garhwal managed to capture Butur-Dograndi after suffering heavy casualties including the loss of their Commanding Officer Lieutenant Colonel J.E. Jhirad. However, Butur-Dograndi was hotly contested by both sides and changed hands several times with the enemy ultimately retaking part of the position. 43 Lorried Brigade was then ordered to launch its attack on Chawinda on 17 September. However, as the troops were far back and could not turn up on time, the attack was called off. During the tank battle Lieutenant Colonel A.B. Tarapore of 17 Horse was killed. He led his regiment with great distinction and gallantry and inflicted considerable tank losses on the enemy. He was awarded the Param Vir Chakra (posthumous).

Citation

Lieutenant Colonel A.B. Tarapore,
POONA HORSE (17 HORSE) (IC 5565)

On 11 September 1965, the Poona Horse Regiment under the command of Lieutenant Colonel Ardeshir Burzarji Tarapore was assigned the task of delivering the main armoured thrust for capturing Phillora in the Sialkot Sector in Pakistan. As a preliminary to making a surprise attack on Phillora from the rear, the regiment was thrusting between Phillora and Chawinda when it was suddenly counter-attacked by the enemy's heavy armour from Wazirali. Lieutenant Colonel A.B. Tarapore who was then at the head of his regiment, defied the enemy's charge, held his ground and gallantly attacked Phillora with one of his squadrons supported by an infantry battalion. Though under continuous enemy tank and artillery fire, Lieutenant Colonel Tarapore remained unperturbed throughout this action and when wounded refused to be evacuated.

On 14 September 1965, though still wounded he again led his regiment to capture Wazirali. Such was his grit and determination that unmindful of his injury, he again gallantly led his regiment and captured Jassoran and Butur-Dograndi on 16 September. His own tank was hit several times, but despite the odds he maintained his pivots in both these places and thereby allowed the supporting infantry to attack Chawinda from the rear.

Inspired by his leadership, the regiment fiercely attacked the enemy's heavy armour destroying approximately 60 enemy tanks at a cost of only 9 tank casualties, and when Lieutenant Colonel A.B. Tarapore was mortally wounded the regiment continue to defy the enemy.

The valour displayed by Lieutenant Colonel A.B. Tarapore in this heroic action which lasted six days was in keeping with the highest traditions of the Indian Army.

Gazette of India Notification
No. 112—Press/65

* * *

Valour To The Fore

Let us have faith that right makes might and in that faith, let us, to the end, dare to do our duty as we understand it.

– Abraham Lincoln

The antecedents of Lieutenant Colonel A.B. Tarapore are very Indian and very military. His ancestor, Ratanjiba, eight generations earlier, was a military leader under Shivaji. In appreciation of his services, loyalty, and bravery, Shivaji had given him the '*Mansab*' (charge) of one hundred villages. The premier village in this Mansab was called Tarapur and it is since then that the family name of Tarapur came into use.

Ardeshir's grandfather migrated to the Deccan and joined the Customs Department of the erstwhile Hyderabad State. Ardeshir's father also joined the same department. He was an erudite scholar of Persian and Urdu.

Ardeshir (Adi) was born at Bombay on 18 August 1923. At the young age of six he demonstrated the courage he was to show in future years when he saved his sister from a charging cow. At the age of seven he joined Sardar Dastur Boy's School, Poona. Although not an exceptional student academically, he distinguished himself in athletics, gymnastics, boxing, swimming, tennis and cricket and matriculated from the school in 1940 as the school captain.

Adi applied for and was selected for a commission in the Hyderabad State Army and joined the Officers Training School

(OTS) at Golconda. On completion of this training he was sent to OTS Bangalore and commissioned on 1st January 1942 in the 7th Hyderabad Infantry. He had however set his heart on joining the armoured regiment of the Hyderabad State Forces which in those days was equipped with Scout cars. An incident took place which helped him realise his dream. His battalion was being inspected by Major General El-Edroos, the Commander-in-Chief of the State Forces. Adi was carrying out routine training at the Grenade Throwing Range when a recruit failed to throw the grenade correctly and it fell back into the throwing bay. Adi immediately jumped into the throwing bay, picked up the grenade and threw it to safety. The grenade burst in midair and he was peppered with splinters in his chest. General El-Edroos summoned Adi to his office after he had recovered from his injuries and personally congratulated him for his courage and presence of mind and asked him if there was anything that he could do for him. Adi requested him for a transfer to the armoured regiment which was accepted and he was transferred to the 1st Hyderabad Imperial Service Lancers.

During World War II, the 1st Hyderabad Lancers saw service in the Middle East. The Commanding Officer of the regiment, a Britisher, was in the habit of speaking in a derogatory manner about Indian soldiers to which Adi one day very strongly objected. This incident assumed serious proportions and was resolved only with the personal intervention of Major General El-Edroos with General Montgomery but it shows Adi's moral courage and the commitment to his soldiers and his regiment.

After the merger of Hyderabad State with the Union of India, Adi was selected to serve in the Indian Army, and was posted to the Poona Horse on probation for two years. He first joined 'B' Squadron and later on 'A' Squadron as its second-in-command. Adi took to 'A' Squadron as a fish takes to water, and soon established a close rapport with the proud tradition-bound Rajputs as he himself was a firm believer in tradition. His behaviour with them was very correct yet friendly, understanding and caring and he soon won their loyalty and affection. He believed that rules and regulations were essential for good discipline but that when necessary they could be broken. Because of his enthusiasm and hard work he was selected for a course in the UK on the newly acquired Centurion tank. In the regiment he acquired the reputation of being a committed, steady, methodical, loyal and courageous commander.

In the 1965 Indo-Pakistan war he fought at the head of his regiment, Poona Horse, in the Sialkot Sector and led it courageously and aggressively for the capture of Phillora against vastly superior numbers of Pakistani armour. He was injured on 14 September 1965 in a fierce tank battle in which a large number of Pakistani tanks were destroyed. He however refused to be evacuated on account of his wounds and continued to lead his regiment offensively against the enemy till he was wounded once again on 16 September 1965 and succumbed to his wounds.

Conclusion of the Indo-Pakistan War

Although many have termed the result of the 1965 war with Pakistan a stalemate it would be more appropriate to say that it was Pakistan who lost the war. Pakistan failed miserably in her aim of annexing Jammu and Kashmir although all factors were heavily loaded in her favour—politically, economically and militarily. On the contrary it resulted in the near total destruction of one of her armoured divisions.

In facing the Pakistani offensive, India decided that the best alternative open to her was the destruction of Pakistani offensive forces and in this she substantially succeeded. The timely occupation of the Asal Uttar position and the conduct of its brave defenders like Company Quartermaster Havildar Abdul Hamid of 4 Grenadiers and the brave and courageous leadership displayed by Lieutenant Colonel A.B. Tarapore of 17 Horse and others like them turned the tide of the war.

It is the leadership and courage of brave men such as these, that sometimes change the course of history and the destiny of nations.

CHAPTER IV

THE
INDO-PAKISTAN WAR
1971

1971
Indo–Pakistan War
Birth of Bangladesh

■

The War in the East

The enemy must be made to dance to your tune and to react to your thrusts.

– Field Marshal B. Montgomery

Ever since the creation of Pakistan, her Western Province had relentlessly usurped the authority and resources of her Eastern partner. In the elections held on 7 December 1970, however, the Awami League led by Sheikh Mujibur Rehman won a landslide victory and emerged as the majority party. Dismayed and disconcerted by this unexpected result, Zulfiqar Ali Bhutto, and Yahya Khan, colluded to prevent domination of Pakistan by a Bengali majority at all cost. Their first step was to postpone the Assembly session. This infuriated the Bengalis and the simmering discontent of decades of oppression broke loose. All government and semi-government offices, central and provincial, closed and students and agitated crowds took to the streets. Curfew was imposed in Dhaka but by 3 March 1971, Mujib's writ ran wide in East Pakistan. Lieutenant General Sahibzada Yakub Khan, the Lieutenant Governor and Martial Law Administrator of East Pakistan was recalled when he refused to massacre unarmed civilians, and was replaced by Lieutenant General Tikka Khan who was to become known as the notorious 'Butcher of Bangladesh'. Tikka Khan let loose a reign of terror and destruction the likes of which have few parallels, in what became infamous as *Operation Blitz*.

The armed forces of Pakistan used machine-guns, tanks and artillery against unarmed civilians and against Bengali paramilitary forces. *Operation Blitz* triggered off a mass exodus of terrified civilians into India. Their number eventually totalled over ten million. Their shelter, food, medical, hygiene and sanitation needs became the responsibility of the Government of India. The burden of refugee relief was estimated at over $700 million. Indian protests were not heeded by Pakistan, the U.N. or the Western powers. Besides the intolerable economic burden, it created grave security problems. These consequences, economic, political and military were not sustainable by India.

When repeated attempts to find a reasonable solution with Pakistan failed, India sought the assistance of the international community to persuade Pakistan to see reason. The West, led by the United States was however indifferent to the plight of the citizens of East Pakistan and the Indian dilemma. Pakistan was their protege and they turned a blind eye to the genocide being perpetrated by her against her own citizens of the Eastern wing. They stated that it was an internal problem of Pakistan and therefore did not warrant their intervention. The refugee problem they stated was India's problem and a solution had to be found bilaterally between India and Pakistan.

India now stood alone in her predicament against the studied indifference of an essentially partisan world and the malevolent machinations of an insolent and arrogant neighbour. The influx of refugees continued. An agitated Indian public now began to demand immediate military action against Pakistan, but the time was not ripe. There were valid reasons against early intervention—political, military, economic and climatic that demanded a self-imposed delay.

A review was carried out that took into account India's state of arms and ammunition, equipment, training, commerce and industry, road and rail communication, climate, weather, morale, world-opinion and enemy options. All these factors pointed to a particular timetable for war that would be suitable to India. Indian leaders heeded this and adhered to this programme and the armed forces used the intervening period to gear up for the expected Pakistani offensive. Pakistan, as expected, did launch her offensive against India on 3 December 1971. By that time, the nation was well prepared.

The planning and conduct of this war by India makes a fascinating story but this is not the place to tell it. Suffice it to say that Indian planners pushed through an excellent strategy that was ably executed by well-trained and highly motivated troops. The timetable was tight. Interference by the United States led by President Nixon was anticipated, but before the US Seventh Fleet could arrive in the Bay of Bengal, the war was concluded. More than 93,000 Pakistani prisoners were taken, a region liberated and a new nation was born. Three Param Vir Chakras were awarded in this war to the Army. One on the Eastern front and two on the West. Lance Naik Albert Ekka of 14 Guards in the East and Major Hoshiar Singh 3 Grenadiers and Second Lieutenant Arun Khetarpal of 17 Horse in the West. The fourth Param Vir Chakra was awarded to an Air Force Officer, Nirmal Jit Sekhon who fought a valiant battle against overwhelming odds over Srinagar. Stories of these intrepid individuals follow.

Lance Naik Albert Ekka
14 GUARDS

The Battle of Gangasagar

In the Eastern Sector, the Indian Army launched an offensive against East Pakistan after Pakistan had launched her offensive in the West. The Indian offensive went along four thrust lines. Our story is about Albert Ekka of 14 Guards, one of the battalions of 4 Corps. The task given to 14 Guards was the containment and capture of Gangasagar which was important because it controlled three major axes and its capture therefore was essential for furtherance of the operations of 4 Corps.

14 Guards moved cross-country and established itself just south of Gangasagar which was located 4 kilometres from Akhaura railway station and formed part of its defences. The main defences were based on the high ground around the railway station and the built-up area. The surrounding marshy area and the few remaining areas were heavily mined with anti-tank and anti-personnel mines. The main defences were also extensively wired. The enemy had used their time well and converted the Gangasagar defences into a strong fortress. Information about the enemy was scant. According to military intelligence, Gangasagar was said to be held by one company. The Mukti Fauj stated that the position was held by a battalion. It was eventually found to have been held by approximately three companies of 12 Frontier Force, a company of 12 Azad Kashmir and reinforced by a company of Razakars.

During patrolling, 14 Guards observed that the enemy was moving freely along the railway track which meant that they were not mined. Two companies of the battalion therefore attacked the enemy defences along the railway track and were able to reach close to them, but when they were approximately 100 yards away, the enemy opened up with heavy automatic fire. Being restricted to the railway lines, heavy casualties would have resulted if the attack wavered. Fired by their determination to complete their task, the companies rose to the occasion and hurled themselves at the enemy defences. The mines and wire took their toll but the remainder assaulted the position and were soon engaged in hand-to-hand fighting. It was at this stage that Lance Naik Albert Ekka who was with one of the forward companies undertook to inscribe his name forever in the annals of the history of his regiment and the nation's roll of honour.

With the enemy entrenched in strong, heavily wired concrete defences the only way to flush them out was by lobbing grenades through the loopholes and finishing them off with the bayonet. One particular light machine-gun (LMG) was holding up the company's progress. Lance Naik Albert Ekka realising the necessity of eliminating this LMG charged the bunker and though seriously wounded in the stomach continued his charge, bayonetted the two enemy soldiers and captured the LMG. Refusing to be evacuated Lance Naik Albert Ekka continued with the assault. Once more it was held up, this time by a medium machine-gun (MMG) which was bringing down heavy and effective fire on his company from a building causing heavy casualties. Lance Naik Albert Ekka climbed a side wall, lobbed a grenade through a loophole and bayonetted the soldier manning the MMG thereby silencing it and permitting his company to capture the objective. In the process, however, he was once again wounded and having carried out his task, succumbed to his injuries. Lance Naik Albert Ekka was posthumously awarded the only Param Vir Chakra awarded in operations in the East in the 1971 war for valour and dedication to duty of the highest order.

Citation

Lance Naik Albert Ekka
14 GUARDS (NO. 4239746)

Lance Naik Albert Ekka was in the left forward company of a battalion of the Brigade of Guards during their attack on the enemy defences at Gangasagar on the Eastern front. This was a well-fortified position held in strength by the enemy. The assaulting troops were subjected to intense shelling and heavy small-arms fire, but they charged onto the objective and were locked in bitter hand-to-hand combat. Lance Naik Albert Ekka noticed an enemy light machine-gun (LMG) inflicting heavy casualties on his company. With complete disregard for his personal safety, he charged the enemy bunker, bayonetted two enemy soldiers and silenced the LMG. Though seriously wounded in this encounter, he continued to fight alongside his comrades through the mile deep objective, clearing bunker after bunker with undaunted courage. Towards the northern end of the objective one enemy medium machine-gun (MMG) opened up from the second storey of a well-fortified building inflicting heavy casualties and holding up the attack. Once again this gallant soldier, without a thought for his personal safety, despite his serious injury and the heavy volume of enemy fire, crawled forward till he reached the building and lobbed a grenade into the bunker killing one enemy soldier and injuring the other. The MMG however continued to fire. With outstanding courage and determination Lance Naik Albert Ekka scaled a side wall and entering the bunker, bayonetted the enemy soldier who was still firing and thus silenced the machine-gun, saving further casualties to his company and ensuring the success of the attack. In this process however, he received serious injuries and succumbed to them after the capture of the objective.

In this action, Lance Naik Albert Ekka displayed the most conspicuous valour and determination and made the supreme sacrifice in the best traditions of the Army.

Gazette of India Notification
No. 7—Press/72

* * *

His Finest Hour

Real leaders are ordinary people with extraordinary determination.

— Charles de Gaulle

No 4237746 Lance Naik Albert Ekka, son of Julius and Mariam Ekka was born and brought up in a village in Bihar. He belonged to an Adivasi tribe in Ranchi and was a devout Christian. From his early days Albert was fond of hunting and like most Adivasis was adept in the art of tracking and hunting with bow and arrow. He was also good at games. His love for adventure and his skills in the jungle helped to make him an excellent soldier, skilful in the use of ground and movement.

Albert developed into a strong healthy young man and was keen to join the army because he loved a life packed with action and adventure. Albert Ekka was enrolled in 1962 in the Bihar Regiment.

Nothing could have made him happier. For him it was a dream come true. When 14 Guards was raised, Albert Ekka with many of his friends was transferred to this unit, which was employed in counter-insurgency duties in the North East. Albert Ekka soon came to the notice of his superiors due to his high skills in marksmanship and battle-craft and his excellence in hockey. During training for a likely war against Pakistan, he was promoted Lance Naik.

His extraordinary commitment and devotion to duty and his bravery and courage of the highest order in the battle of Gangasagar earned him the posthumous award of the Param Vir Chakra, India's highest award for gallantry in the face of the enemy.

The War in the West
Major Hoshiar Singh

3 GRENADIERS

The term 'West' is used to differentiate it from operations in East Pakistan. The war in the 'West' was fought in the Northern, Western and Southern command regions.

Two Param Vir Chakras were awarded in the 'West' during the 1971 Indo-Pakistan War for bravery displayed by two officers—Major Hoshiar Singh of 3 Grenadiers and Second Lieutenant Arun Khetarpal of 17 Horse in the battle of Basantar—a fiercely contested battle that took place when our forces launched an offensive against the Shakargarh Bulge in the plains sector opposite Jammu and Kashmir.

The Shakargarh Bulge was of strategic importance to both India and Pakistan. To India it was important because its capture would not only remove the threat to Jammu and Kashmir and Northern Punjab, but would also enable India to pose a threat to the heartland of Pakistan. To Pakistan it was important because it facilitated an offensive against the Indian base at Pathankot, the capture of which would isolate Jammu and Kashmir.

Being aware of its strategic importance Pakistan had constructed an elaborate network of obstacles and a continuous anti-tank ditch between the Chenab river and the Degh Nadi. Further east, the Supwal Ditch linked up with the Basantar river. All the major towns namely Zafarwal, Dhamtal, Quila Soba Singh, and Narowal had anti-tank ditches in front of them and these were inter-linked to form a continuous belt from the Degh Nadi to the Ravi river. To further strengthen these obstacles, Pakistan had laid extensive minefields in depth.

54 Infantry Division as part of its operations, had to establish a bridgehead across the Basantar river, capture the Supwal Ditch and then regroup for the capture of Zafarwal and other objectives.

On 15 and 16 December the brigades of 54 Infantry Division launched their attacks. At 1050 hours on 16 December, Pakistan counter-attacked with strong forces of infantry and armour and a major tank battle developed. Between 16 and 17 December, Pakistan launched no less than six fierce counter-attacks and suffered heavy losses that included the loss of 46 tanks. At 1810 hours on 17 December the enemy launched its sixth counter-attack against 3 Grenadiers. It was in these operations that Major Hoshiar Singh of 3 Grenadiers and Second Lieutenant Arun Khetarpal of 17 Horse were awarded Param Vir Chakras for gallantry of the most exceptional order. These two awards are unique because it was the first time that two Param Vir Chakras were awarded for the same battle to two different units. Second Lieutenant Arun Khetarpal was also the youngest person of the armed forces to have been given this award. He had only six months service when he was killed in action.

Was it a strange coincidence that Poona Horse and 3 Grenadiers were brought together once again at the battle of Basantar to renew old bonds forged together at the Battle of Koregaon in 1818? Both units were part of the Army of the erstwhile Bombay Presidency. Stranger still, 13 Lancers, the Pakistani Armoured Regiment that faced Poona Horse at this same battle, each doing their best to destroy each other also belonged to the erstwhile Bombay Army!

The Battle of Basantar

One of the fiercest battles in the Western Sector was fought in the 900 square kilometre Shakargarh Bulge where two of the four

Param Vir Chakras of the 1971 conflict were awarded. The overall plan was to gain some ground for the defence of the Pathankot-Jammu road which runs dangerously close to the border with Pakistan. The entire area is full of natural obstacles which were augmented by extensive Pakistani anti-tank minefields.

On 14 December 1971, Commanding Officer 3 Grenadiers was given orders to lead the assault of a brigade attack on the Supwal Ditch. 3 Grenadiers was to capture Lohal and Jarpal villages. The battle of Jarpal was to subsequently assume historical importance as a battle where two sub-unit commanders of two different units of the Indian Army won the Param Vir Chakra in the same battle and where the attacking battalion commander of the opposing side was awarded the Hilal-e-Jurat, Pakistan's second highest gallantry award. Major Hoshiar Singh of 3 Grenadiers and Second Lieutenant Arun Khetarpal of 17 Horse (Poona Horse) were both awarded the Param Vir Chakra. Part of the plan was an outflanking move to isolate the Supwal Ditch defences by capturing Jarpal which was to its rear. The minefield protecting the objective was 1200 yards deep.

At last light 15 December 1971, two companies, one led by Major Hoshiar Singh, launched the first phase of the attack. Both companies captured their objectives in the face of heavy artillery and machine-gun fire. They reported capture of twenty prisoners of war and large quantities of arms and ammunition including RCL and MMG guns. At first light 16 December, a squadron of 17 Horse less two troops joined 3 Grenadiers, renewing an old bond between the two regiments forged at the Battle of Koregaon in 1818.

This day, 16 December saw the fiercest fighting in the Sector. 3 Grenadiers and the armour in its support were repeatedly counter-attacked by wave after wave of determined enemy infantry and armour. Second Lieutenant Arun Khetarpal of 17 Horse was killed fighting very courageously and was awarded the Param Vir Chakra posthumously.

3 Grenadiers meanwhile rose to the occasion beating back repeated counter-attacks by the enemy and breaking up assault after assault by accurate fire. Morale was high and cheerful cries flew between trenches as soldiers and sub-unit commanders encouraged each other, marked and engaged enemy targets and took a very heavy toll of the attackers.

On 17 December, just before first light, the enemy battalion commander leading his battalion and armour in person launched another determined attack on Major Hoshiar Singh's company. Calm and undeterred, Major Hoshiar Singh fought very aggressively inspiring his men with his own confidence and zest for battle. Though wounded, he moved from trench to trench, encouraging his men to defeat the repeated and relentless Pakistani counter-attacks. He himself manned the MMG guns when the MMG gunner was killed. His company thus motivated, encouraged and brought very effective fire on the enemy, decimating the assaulting battalion. That day, the enemy left 89 dead on the battlefield, including their intrepid Commanding Officer, Lieutenant Colonel Mohammed Akram Raja, 35 Frontier Force Rifles and three of his officers.

Throughout the rest of the day the remnants of the assaulting battalion, 35 Frontier Force Rifles, kept exchanging fire with 3 Grenadiers. At 1800 hours, orders were received that a ceasefire was scheduled for 2000 hours. Both battalions thereupon brought maximum fire on each other. By the time the ceasefire was declared 3 Grenadiers had lost one officer and 32 men killed and 3 officers, 4 Junior Commissioned Officers, and 86 men wounded. The Battle Honour of Jarpal was subsequently awarded to the battalion.

After the ceasefire, the body of Lieutenant Colonel Mohammed Akram Raja, the Commanding Officer 35 Frontier Force Rifles along with 88 others who fell with him were handed over to the Pakistani Brigade Commander, Brigadier Shah Baz Khan. Colonel Ved Airy, Commanding Officer 3 Grenadiers also handed over a citation extolling the courage and fighting spirit of his gallant opponent. It was later learnt that based on this citation, Lieutenant Colonel Mohammed Akram Raja earned the award of the Hilal-e-Jurat, Pakistan's second highest award for gallantry. Such a chivalrous gesture towards one's adversary in battle and its immediate response is indeed remarkable and one seldom comes across such incidents in the history of warfare.

* * *

Citation

Major Hoshiar Singh
3 GRENADIERS (IC—14608)

On 15 December 1971 a battalion of the Grenadiers was given the task of establishing a bridgehead across the Basantar river in the Shakargarh Sector. Major Hoshiar Singh was commanding the left forward company and he was ordered to capture the enemy locality of Jarpal. This was a well-fortified position and was held in strength by the enemy. During the assault, his company came under intense shelling and effective crossfire from enemy medium machine guns. Undeterred, he led the charge and captured the objective after a fierce hand-to-hand fight. The enemy reacted and put in three counter attacks on 16 December 1971, two of them supported by armour. Major Hoshiar Singh unmindful of the heavy shelling and tank fire went from trench to trench, motivating his command and encouraging his men to stand fast and fight. Inspired by his courage and dauntless leadership, his company repulsed all the attacks inflicting heavy casualties on the enemy. Again, on 17 December 1971 the enemy made another attack with a battalion supported by heavy artillery fire. Though seriously wounded by enemy shelling, Major Hoshiar Singh again went from trench to trench moving about in the open with utter disregard to his personal safety when an enemy shell landed near the medium machine gun post injuring the crew and rendering it inoperative. Major Hoshiar Singh, realising the importance of machine-gun fire, immediately rushed to the machine-gun pit and though seriously wounded himself, manned the gun inflicting heavy casualties on the enemy. The attack was successfully repulsed and the enemy retreated leaving behind 85 dead including their Commanding Officer and three other officers. Though seriously wounded, Major Hoshiar Singh refused to be evacuated till the ceasefire.

Throughout this operation, Major Hoshiar Singh displayed most conspicuous gallantry, indomitable fighting spirit and leadership in the highest traditions of the Army.

Gazette of India Notification
No. 7—Press/72

* * *

The Legend and the Man

It is not the numbers of soldiers, but their will to win which decides battles.

– Unknown

Hoshiar Singh was born on 5 May 1936 in village Sisana in the Sonepat district of Haryana.

His early life was spent in the village where he went to the local school and later to the Jat Higher Secondary School. He was a good student and secured a First Division in his matriculation examination. He was also an outstanding sportsman and at a very young age was selected to represent the combined Punjab team in volleyball at the National championships. He later captained the Punjab team and was selected for the National team.

It was at one of these volleyball matches that he was spotted by one of the senior officials of the Jat Regimental Centre who persuaded him to join the Jat Regiment. He was enrolled in 2 Jat in 1957 and later on commissioned into 3 Grenadiers.

His courage, drive and determination in operations was noticed during the 1965 War in the Bikaner Sector when mounted a camel and disguised as a civilian, he carried out aggressive patrolling for the battalion and brought back valuable information which was instrumental in ensuring the success of the battalion operation. He was mentioned-in-despatches for his initiative and courage.

Hoshiar Singh was a born leader. He was also filled with the desire to overcome all odds and to come out on top. His personal charisma and ability to succeed in all that he attempted to do, inspired his men who would follow him through thick and thin and no sacrifice was too great for him or for them. He demonstrated these qualities not only in war, as in the battle of Basantar but also in peace. During his tenure as a Company Commander at the Indian Military Academy, his company remained the overall champion company for six consecutive terms—a record that remains unbroken till today and is unlikely to ever be broken.

Colonel Hoshiar Singh's life is an example of the triumph of the will and spirit over all obstacles.

Citation of Lieutenant Colonel Mohammed Akram Raja

35 FRONTIER FORCE RIFLES (PAKISTAN ARMY)

Written by Lieutenant Colonel Ved Airy Commanding Officer 3 Grenadiers

Lieutenant Colonel Mohammed Akram Raja, Officer Commanding 35 Frontier Force Rifles who led the counter-attack on Indian position of village Jarpal at 0400 hrs on 17 December 1971 has died a real soldier's death. Our hats off to him.

He was personally leading the attack by being in the front line of assault, when he was hit by an MMG burst right on the face killing him on the spot.

We had recovered his body on 18 December 1971 after having been told by one of the prisoners of war captured by us. The prisoner also helped us in identifying the dead body. We found both his arms frozen after death, in the position in which he was holding his Sten gun which indicates his determination to get ahead.

In this action, Lieutenant Colonel Mohammed Akram Raja displayed courage, determination and personal bravery of the highest order in keeping with the tradition of soldiers.

This brave deed of Lieutenant Colonel Raja a brave soldier, should not go unnoticed.

Praying for the departed soul.

Field
December '71

Lieutenant Colonel
(V.P. Airy)

* * *

Citation

Second Lieutenant Arun Khetarpal
POONA HORSE (IC-25067)

On 16 December 1971, the Squadron Commander of 'B' Squadron, the Poona Horse asked for reinforcements as the Pakistani armour which was superior in strength, counter-attacked at Jarpal, in the Shakargarh Sector. On hearing this transmission, Second Lieutenant Arun Khetarpal who was in 'A' Squadron, voluntarily moved along with his troop, to assist the other squadron. En route, while crossing the Basantar river, Second Lieutenant Arun Khetarpal and his troop came under fire from enemy strong points and RCL gun nests that were still holding out. Time was at a premium and as a critical situation was developing in the 'B' Squadron sector, Second Lieutenant Arun Khetarpal, threw caution to the winds and started attacking the impending enemy strong points by literally charging them, overrunning the defence works with his tanks and capturing the enemy infantry and weapon crews at pistol point. In the course of one such daring attack one tank commander of his troop was killed. Second Lieutenant Arun Khetarpal continued to attack relentlessly until all enemy opposition was overcome and he broke through towards the 'B' Squadron position, just in time to see the enemy tanks pulling back after their initial probing

attack on this squadron. He was so carried away by the wild enthusiasm of battle and the impetus of his own headlong dash that he started chasing the withdrawing tanks and even managed to shoot and destroy one. Soon thereafter, the enemy reformed with a squadron of armour for a second attack and this time they selected the sector held by Second Lieutenant Arun Khetarpal and two other tanks as the point for their main effort. A fierce tank fight ensued: ten enemy tanks were hit and destroyed of which Second Lieutenant Arun Khetarpal personally destroyed four. By this time Second Lieutenant Arun Khetarpal was severely wounded. He was asked by his squadron commander to abandon his tank but realising that the enemy though badly decimated was continuing to advance in his sector of responsibility and that if he abandoned his tank the enemy would break through, he gallantly fought on and destroyed another enemy tank. At this stage his tank received a second hit which resulted in the death of this gallant officer.

Second Lieutenant Arun Khetarpal was dead but he

Arun Khetarpal's mother, Mrs. M.L. Khetarpal receiving her son's posthumous award of the Param Vir Chakra from the President Mr. V.V. Giri at the Republic Day Parade on 26 January 1972.

had, by his intrepid valour saved the day; the enemy was
denied the breakthrough he was so desperately seeking.
Not one enemy tank got through.

Second Lieutenant Arun Khetarpal had shown the
best qualities of leadership, tenacity of purpose and
the will to close in with the enemy. This was an act of
courage and self-sacrifice far beyond the call of duty.

Gazette of India Notification
No. 7—Press/72

* * *

The Boy Hero of 1971

Cannon to right of them,
Cannon to left of them,
Cannon in front of them
Volleyed and thundered.
Stormed at with shot and shell,
Boldly they rode and well,
Into the jaws of Death,
Into the mouth of Hell.

– Alfred Lord Tennyson

Arun Khetarpal belonged to a family with a long tradition of
military service. His great-great grandfather had served in the
Sikh Army and had fought against the British at Chilianwala
in 1848. His grandfather served in the Army during World
War I from 1917 to 1919. Arun's father, Brigadier M.L.
Khetarpal, AVSM served in the Corps of Engineers and took
part in the Indo-Pak war of 1965 as Chief Engineer 1 Corps.
The Khetarpal family belonged to Sargodha, now in Pakistan
and after Partition migrated to India.

Arun was born at Poona on 14 October 1950, and his early schooling took place wherever his father was posted. He spent the last five years at Lawrence School, Sanawar. Arun was good at both academics and games. He played cricket for the school team. He was a Squadron Cadet Captain at the National Defence Academy and a Senior Under Officer at the Indian Military Academy at Dehra Dun. He passed out from the IMA on 13 June 1971.

Arun joined the Poona Horse in June 1971. As is customary in the regiment, young officers are made to work their way up from driver, gunner, radio operator, crew commander to troop leader. Arun cheerfully carried out whatever task he was assigned. When he took charge as driver of his tank he devoted himself totally to its care, cleanliness and maintenance. He was very fond of the men and was completely at home with them whether at work or play. Off parade, Arun was full of life and had a delightful sense of humour.

An excellent insight into Arun's character comes through in a letter from his father to an officer of the Armoured Corps.

I am giving below a few extracts from memory . . .

General S.D. Verma, Poona Horse wrote to me on 15 February 1972 after visiting the Regiment then still in Pakistan: 'I have been to the spot where his tank was and where he was not prepared to abandon his comrades both of infantry and armour. He died a soldier's death. I would have gladly given away ten years of my life to see him personally receive the award he deserved ten times over for his selfless conduct.'

Lieutenant General Har Prasad wrote to me in February 1972: 'You had requested me to get Arun posted to Poona

Horse which I did. The boy got the regiment of his choice—
but at what cost!'

At the IMA, Arun, (a Senior Under Officer) was on one
occasion given two contradictory orders, one to report at the
Firing Range at 1100 hours. The second order said, 'You
will attend a Library meeting at 1100 hours.' He chose to
go to the Firing Range. He was hauled up for failing to be
at the Library. Consequently, he was reverted to the ranks
from his post of SUO. Arun got his rank back subsequently
but discipline had to be maintained!

I have a letter from Arun dated 10 December 1971 written
while ten miles inside Pakistan territory: 'Dear Daddy, we
are having a damned good time! Our regiment is at the top
of the world. Soon we will finish the war.'

Yes, the war was over on 17 December. For Arun too.
He left this world on 16 December.

From the above incidents/letters, you can see inside Arun's
personality. He wanted to be posted to Poona Horse; he lived
like a Poona Horse officer, and he died like one . . . but that
was 30 years ago. Seems like yesterday.

With kind regards

Yours sincerely

Madan Khetarpal.

Six feet two inches tall, Arun was young, strong, capable and
impressionable. What strikes one is the commitment and
dedication to his profession, his straightforward approach
to life and his truthfulness irrespective of the consequences.
Brave and courageous he set a personal example in all that he
did. The war brought out the best in him and his leadership
and decisiveness are evident in the way he conducted himself
during battle. He was the ideal young officer and was marked

for greater things in life. However, fate in the form of the 1971 war intervened and took him away to a different destiny. Arun was only 21 years old and he had just six months service.

When Arun Khetarpal's tank was hit and caught fire, his commander ordered him to abandon the burning tank. Arun however realising how important it was to prevent a breakthrough of enemy armour in this area, refused to do so. His last transmission was 'No Sir, I will not abandon my tank. My gun is still working and I will get these . . .' The last enemy tank which he destroyed was just 100 metres away from him. At this point his tank received a second hit and was destroyed. Arun may have died in the achievement of his mission but his inspiring example stirs the hearts and minds of all those who read his story. His life and the manner of his dying will motivate future generations of officers for all time to come.

The Strange Sequel

The Indo-Pakistan War of 1971 is now history. More than 30 years have gone by since the day Second Lieutenant Arun Khetarpal, PVC, fought at the battle of Basantar and gave his all for regiment and country. However, for the Khetarpal family the story did not end here. A strange sequel was to follow.

Many years after the 1971 War with Pakistan, a series of meetings between retired officers of the armed forces and bureaucrats of both countries started taking place in an attempt to improve 'people-to-people' contact between the two nations. This effort came to be known as 'Twin Track Diplomacy' and in the process, officials of both countries crossed borders to discuss how the peoples of both countries could come closer together.

After some time, Brigadier M.L. Khetarpal, the father of Arun Khetarpal, began getting messages from across the border through officials of the twin track diplomatic effort that a certain brigadier from Pakistan would like to meet him.

The name of the officer was, however, unfamiliar to Brigadier Khetarpal and so he did not make any attempt to encourage the meeting. This matter would have ended here had a further development not taken place.

In the year 2001, Brigadier Khetarpal, now 81 years old desired to have one last look at the place where he was born. This was at Sargodha, now in Pakistan. It was a wish he thought would never materialise but which he gave voice to, when conversing with one of the officers who had participated in the twin track diplomatic visits. This officer assured Brigadier Khetarpal that he would help him make the requisite applications, which would however require the sanction of both governments. A visa to visit Pakistan was subsequently obtained. Brigadier Khetarpal was told that he would be met at Lahore and that arrangements for his visit to Sargodha had been made.

On landing at Lahore Airport, Brigadier Khetarpal was met by Brigadier Khawja Mohamad Naser who took it upon himself to be Brigadier Khetarpal's host and guide. This officer went out of his way to ensure that every detail of Brigadier Khetarpal's visit to his birthplace was attended to. After a very satisfying and nostalgic visit to his old home, Brigadier Khetarpal returned to Lahore where he stayed with his host as an honoured guest for three days. Brigadier Khetarpal was overwhelmed by the extreme kindness, deference, courtesy and respect bestowed upon him by Brigadier Naser, all the members of his family and his many servants.

Some Muslim families are very conservative in their social interaction with outsiders but all doors were opened to Brigadier Khetarpal and he was treated as a close and respected member of the family. As the countdown for his departure progressed, the bonds of friendship between the hosts and their guest grew stronger with every passing day and yet there appeared to be something between them that remained unspoken. Brigadier Khetarpal felt, at times, that something was amiss but could not quite make out what it was. Was it the long silences that punctuated their animated conversations of late? Was it the hint of compassion in the eyes of the women of the household. Brigadier Khetarpal wondered, but he pushed it out of his mind. What was certain, however, was that he would never forget the hospitality, warmth and affection of this Pakistani family who treated him as someone very, very special.

On the day before his departure, the family had dinner together and sat chatting as usual. All details of Brigadier Khetarpal's family were now known to this Pakistani family and gifts were handed over for each member of the family in India.

Finally, it was time to retire for the night when Brigadier Naser said, 'Sir, there is something I have wanted to tell you for many years but did not know how to get through to you and say it. Now finally, when I had given up all hope, fate intervened and sent you to us as our honoured guest. We have come very close to each other these past few days and this has made my task all the more difficult. I have something to tell you and it concerns your son. Arun Khetarpal is a national hero . . .the youngest recipient of the Param Vir Chakra and you and I have become very close friends. But on that fateful day, at the battle of *Bade Pind**, we were soldiers unknown to each other, fighting for the safety and honour of our respective countries. I regret to have to tell you that your son died at my hands. Arun's courage on the battlefield was exemplary and he moved his tank with fearless courage and daring, totally unconcerned about his own safety. Tank casualties on both sides were very heavy, till finally it was just the two of us who faced each other. We both fired simultaneously... it was destined that I was to live and that he had to die. It was only later that I came to know who he was and how young he was. We are trained to fight and to kill without pity or remorse. War is something impersonal. We do in war what we have to do, without thinking too much about it but besides

---

* Known to the Indian Army as the Battle of Basantar

being soldiers we are also human and sometimes war takes a personal turn and makes an impact on the inner self. This is one such incident. I had all along thought I would ask for your forgiveness but I will not do that because in the telling of this story I realise that there is nothing to forgive. Instead, I salute your son for what he was and what he did at such a young age and meeting you I salute you too because I understand how he grew into such a fine young man. In the ultimate analysis it is character and values that matter.'

Brigadier Khetarpal listened to this revelation quietly. Silence was his only response to an overwhelming sadness that filled his being. To be faced with the man who killed his son was difficult enough—but to be his guest and the recipient of his hospitality was mortifying. And yet the man was genuinely wanting, in some way, to compensate for something he only did in the line of duty. Ruminating on the turn of events he realised that doing one's duty in war, in the heat of the moment, is easier than reflecting on the consequences later on in life. Soldiers do understand that for them life and death are two sides of the same coin. Fate and circumstance do indeed circumscribe a soldier's destiny but again destiny is not entirely a matter of chance but is dependent on the choices one makes. The soldier must do what he has been trained to do unhesitatingly and with full resolve and determination. Officers, more than men, have to take control and do what is right. The fate of a battle often hangs in balance and it is those who lead decisively irrespective of consequence who are able to tilt the scales and snatch victory from the jaws of defeat. The battle of Basantar was a critical battle and Arun played an important part in preventing the Pakistani armoured regiment from breaking through. In doing so, he came through with honour for family, regiment and country. Although he was very young, his outstanding leadership saved the day and the last witness to his heroic bravery was this man in front of him who also only did his duty. What greater tribute could there be to a man's courage in war than an accolade from the foe stating that his son's conduct as a soldier was outstanding?

The Brigadiers retired for the night, each with his own thoughts, underscored perhaps by the futility of war. After all, there are no victors in war—both sides lose, and it is the families who have to pay the price and suffer the most. As someone said—'Wars are caused by politicians, compounded by bureaucrats and fought by soldiers.' In the ultimate analysis, however, it is how a soldier conducts himself in battle that is most important to his self-esteem and to his standing amongst his peers. What matters most is honour. Arun's conduct in battle was impeccable and it was not only confirmed by the nation's highest award for gallantry but also by the acknowledgement by a member of the opposing force who played a critical part in the battle. For a soldier nothing more needed to be said and it was best that matters were allowed to rest here.

The next day photographs were taken in the garden and Brigadier Khetarpal returned to his home in Delhi. Later on, the photographs reached Delhi. At the back of one of them was a note from Brigadier Naser that said:

With warmest regards
and utmost sincerity

To
Brigadier Khetarpal father of
Shaheed Second Lieutenant Arun Khetarpal, PVC
who stood like an unsurmountable rock
between the victory and failure of the counter-attack
by the 'SPEARHEADS' 13 LANCERS on 16 December 1971
in the battle of 'Bara Pind' as we call it and battle
of 'Basantar' as 17 Poona Horse remembers

Khawja Mohamad Naser, 13 Lancers
Dated 02 March 2001, Lahore

Brig. M.L Khetarpal Indian Army father of Arun Khetarpal, PVC and Brig. K.M. Naser, 13 Lancers Pak Army at Lahore March 2001.

On his return to Delhi, Mrs. Khetarpal asked her husband. 'So, Madan, how was your visit to Pakistan?'

'Good,' was his reply.

What more could he say?

This story is based on the account narrated to the author by Brigadier M.L. Khetarpal, father of Second Lieutenant Arun Khetarpal, PVC.

Before this book was launched, the author asked Brigadier Khetarpal whether he had informed his wife about the revelation made at Lahore by Brigadier K.M. Nasser and what would happen if Mrs. Khetarpal learnt about it only after the release of the book? The Brigadier's answer is worth remembering. He said, 'Remember that Mrs. Khetarpal is an army officer's daughter, an army officer's wife and an army officer's mother. She will understand.'

The Battle for the Sky: Indo–Pak War 1971

Six years after the Indo-Pakistan War of 1965. Pakistan was to initiate war once again. On 3 December 1971, Pakistan launched unprovoked surprise air-attacks on several air-bases in the Western sector. The Indian Air Force was, however, more than equal to this challenge and not a single IAF base was put out of action. The special characteristic of the 1971 war was the excellent coordination and cooperation among the three arms of India's defence forces. This, more than anything else, made a complex campaign that led to the liberation of Bangladesh look so effortless. Complete understanding between the Army and the IAF also effectively halted Pakistan's determined offensive in Chhamb. The Pakistani armoured offensive at Longewala in Rajasthan was also effectively stemmed and ultimately routed by a handful of Hunters and a whole regiment of T-54 tanks was destroyed by air action alone.

In Bangladesh, the IAF achieved total air superiorty within the first 24 hours of the outbreak of hostilities. This enabled it to concentrate undividedly on operations in support of the Army. In order to cut off the withdrawal of Pakistani troops to Dhaka from the Mymensingh area, it was decided to paradrop a battalion of 50 Para Brigade, together with its supporting arms, in the Tangail area. The entire operation was completed with clockwork precision in just 30 minutes. This was the first large-scale para operation undertaken by the IAF in war. The first heli-borne operation was also undertaken by the IAF in 1971 when it heli-lifted 4/5 Gorkha Rifles (Frontier Force) and heli-landed them at Sylhet nearly 100 kilometres behind enemy lines. IAF helicopters were also extensively used by the army for 'air-bridging' the innumerable water obstacles criss-crossing the countryside. This went a long way in speeding up the campaign and reducing casualties. But such operations were made possible only because total command of the air had been achieved by the strike force of the IAF. The capability and effectiveness of the strike force is evident from the precision attack on the conference room in Dhaka which helped hasten the decision of the Pakistani high command to surrender.

In the Western Sector, Srinagar was one of the airfields very frequently attacked by the Pakistani Air Force. No. 18 (Gnat) Squadron was assigned its air defence. On the 14 December, 1971, the airfield was attacked by six Pakistani Sabre jets. Notwithstanding the grave danger of attempting a take-off under such circumstances, Flying Officer Nirmal Jit Singh Sekhon got airborne and engaged the Sabre formation. Then began an unequal contest between the Srinagar Gnat and the six Sabres over Srinagar airfield. Sekhon shot down one Sabre and set another on fire before sheer numbers gained ascendancy and brought him down.

Flying Officer Nirmal Jit Singh Sekhon was awarded the Param Vir Chakra posthumously—the first individual from the IAF to be awarded the highest gallantry award in the country for a pre-eminent act of valour.

The Defence of the Skies over Srinagar

In the Western Sector, Srinagar was one of the airfields frequently attacked by the Pakistani Air Force. Flying Officer Nirmal Jit Singh Sekhon was a pilot of a Gnat detachment based in Srinagar for the air defence of the Valley against Pakistani air attacks.

On 14 December 1971, Srinagar airfield was attacked by a wave of six enemy F-86 Sabre aircraft. Flight Lieutenant B.S. Ghumman and Flying Officer N.J.S. Sekhon were on readiness duty at that time. No dawn observation at the airfield had been mounted because of poor visibility. At 0802 hours on warning from the outlying OPs (Observation Posts) Flight Lieutenant Ghumman and Flying Officer Sekhon were scrambled to intercept the incoming strike. However, about ten seconds were spent in giving the duo clearance to take off. Finally, Flight Lieutenant Ghumman and Flying Officer Sekhon took off without clearance at 0804 hours. By this time, the first of the Sabre jets was commencing its dive over the airfield.

Flight Lieutenant Ghumman was airborne first. As Flying Officer Sekhon took off, the first bombs landed on the runway behind him. While Ghumman turned left immediately after take-off to position himself behind the Sabres, Sekhon who had headed straight after take-off made contact with the two Sabres who had bombed the airfield. By this time the CAP (Combat Air Patrol) controllers had lost contact with Sekhon as the entire sector into which he had gone was obscured by the dust and smoke thrown up by the exploding bombs. The visibility then was about 1 km. The Flight Commander, Squadron Leader V.S. Pathania, VrC, VM caught a glimpse of the two aircraft in close combat. Ghumman tried in vain to assist Sekhon but could not be vectored because of the very poor visibility and the extremely fluid positions of the aircraft in combat. R/T (Radio/Telephony) transmissions received by the CAP control from Sekhon are as follows: 'I am behind two Sabres. I won't let the . . . get away.' A little while later a Gnat gunburst was heard, and one Sabre was seen going out of control with its right wing on fire and trailing thick smoke. Then Sekhon transmitted: 'I am in a Circle of Joy but with two Sabres. I am getting behind one, the other is getting an edge on me.' Squadron Leader Pathania told him to punch his tanks which he had apparently already done. At this stage another Gnat burst was heard followed by a short Sabre burst and again followed by an extremely long Sabre burst. After this Sekhon transmitted, 'I think I've been hit, Ghumman come get them.' This was Sekhon's last transmission.

Flying Officer Sekhon lost his life valiantly fighting against overwhelming odds.

For his supreme valour in the face of the enemy, Flying Officer Sekhon was posthumously awarded the nation's highest gallantry award—the Param Vir Chakra.

* * *

Citation

Flying Officer Nirmal Jit Singh Sekhon
IAF (NO. 10877 F[P])

Flying Officer Nirmal Jit Singh Sekhon was a pilot of a Gnat detachment based at Srinagar for the air defence of the Valley against Pakistani air attacks. From the very outbreak of the hostilities he and his colleagues fought successive waves of intruding Pakistani aircraft with valour and determination, maintaining the high reputation of Gnat aircraft. On 14 December 1971, Srinagar airfield was attacked by a wave of enemy six Sabre aircraft. Flying Officer Sekhon was on readiness duty at the time. Immediately, however, no fewer than six enemy aircraft were overhead, and they began bombing and strafing the airfield. In spite of the mortal danger of attempting to take off during the attack, Flying Officer Sekhon took off and immediately engaged a pair of the attacking Sabres. In the fight that ensued, he secured hits on one aircraft and set another on fire. By this time the other Sabre aircraft came to the aid of their hard-pressed companions and Flying Officer Sekhon's Gnat was again outnumbered, this time by four to one. Even though alone, Flying Officer Sekhon engaged the enemy in an unequal combat. In the fight that followed, at treetop height, he almost held his own, but was eventually overcome by the sheer weight of numbers. His aircraft crashed and he was killed.

The sublime heroism, supreme gallantry, flying skill and determination above and beyond the call of duty displayed by Flying Officer Sekhon in the face of certain death have set new heights in Air Force traditions.

Gazette of India Notification
No. 7—Press/72

* * *

Reaching For The Sky

Success in the game is the great incentive to subdue fear. Once you've shot down two or three, the effect is terrific and you will go on till you are killed . . . '

– Unknown

Nirmal Jit Singh Sekhon was born on 17 July 1945 and belonged to village Rurka Isewal, Ludhiana, Punjab. He was commissioned on 4 June 1967 and was a second generation officer of the Indian Air Force.

Better known as 'Brother' for his ever-helpful and cheerful attitude towards life, Nirmal was well liked by his colleagues in No. 18 (Gnat) Squadron. Nirmal joined the Squadron in October 1968 and had a great deal of experience on the Gnat

He was only 26 years old when he died. He is survived by his wife Manjit Singh Sekhon. They had been married for only a few months and Nirmal Spent most of that time at Srinagar, away from his wife.

Mrs Sekhon has remarried and lives at Chandigarh. Nirmal's father is very old and lives at his village Rurka Isewal in Ludhiana.

Nirmal mirrors the attitude of the typical officer of the Indian Air Force—cool and calm in a crisis, taking each day as it comes and reacting to danger in a positive and professional manner.

Conclusion of the Indo-Pakistan War 1971

*Victory turns on the 'spirit' of armies, 'will' of commanders,
and the 'support' of the civilian national base, not simply the
indiscriminate application of raw force. Let any of the three
components of victory be lacking, and defeat is assured.*
      – Lieutenant Colonel Frederick W Timmerman Jr.

The most remarkable aspect of this war is the manner in which it was planned, executed and brought to a swift conclusion. In the East it was fought across a land that was interspersed with many rivers, with very little river-crossing equipment. In the West, although the strategy adopted was to 'hold', so offensive was our defence that we were able to capture 419 sq miles of enemy territory against a loss of only 42 sq miles. In the Kargil Sector alone, a brigade on its own captured 38 Pakistani picquets. The Indian armed forces executed in the short span of 13 days an impossible task and decimated a formidable enemy taking 93,000 prisoners of war. *The Sunday Times* of London said, 'It took only 13 days for the Indian Army to smash its way to Dhaka, an achievement reminiscent of the German blitzkrieg across France in 1940.'

The price paid was heavy. My own battalion, the 4th Battalion the 5th Gorkha Rifles (FF) started the war with 18 officers and ended it in 13 days with just 7 officers. Four officers were killed and seven wounded. The determination to achieve our objectives and the motivation to wrap up the campaign before foreign intervention was very strong. Service Headquarters had aimed at completing the campaign in 21 days but so determined was the resolve of our men and the Mukti Bahini that even this short period was cut down to just 13 days. When the American Task Force ordered by President Nixon and headed by the nuclear powered 'USS Enterprise' (United States Ship Enterprise) arrived in the Bay of Bengal it was a little too late. The war was over, and Bangladesh was born.

Not to be forgotten is the Indian Navy's victory on the western and eastern sea boards. That however is a separate story.

CHAPTER V

THE
KARGIL WAR MAY–JULY
1999

May–July 1999
The Kargil War

■

The Kargil operation was put on the drawing board by competent military minds many years ago. 'Kargil' was presented as a 'do-able' option when the time was ripe, partly as military revenge for the loss of Siachen and partly as a political device to spur the Kashmiri mujahideen towards greater sacrifice and heroism.

— Editorial, Friday Times *(Pakistan) 1999*

The war in Kargil was Pakistan's third futile attempt to take Kashmir by force. In concept, the plan was diabolically clever, its timing politically astute and in deceit and deception—at which Pakistan is invariably good—it was brilliant.

Pakistan's aim in Kargil was to cut off Kashmir from Ladakh by severing the Srinagar-Leh National Highway, to isolate Kargil, and to terminate India's lifeline to Siachen. The timing of her operation was politically cunning and devious. Even as she was negotiating peace with India after Prime Minister Vajpayee's celebrated bus-ride to Lahore, she was simultaneously pushing in troops across the Line of Control in the furtherance of her aggressive military plans. This in fact puts a firm negative seal on Pakistan's credibility which we hope Indian planners will always keep in mind.

The plan however was not a new one. It is now learnt from Pakistani newspapers that it was conceived more than a decade earlier in 1987 when Zia-ul-Haq was at the helm of affairs. It was, however, shelved because the foreign minister at that time, Lieutenant General Yakub Khan advised Zia-ul-Haq against it, outlining its military, political and diplomatic defects. The plan was, however, revived in 1994 and again in 1997 when Pervez Musharraf was the General Officer Commanding of the corps that had to implement it. It was planned to be put into effect in 1998 but according to the Pakistani newspaper *Nawa-i-waqt*, Jehangir Karamat, the Pakistani Chief of Army Staff, was not willing to push it through and consequently lost his job. The Prime Minister Nawaz Sharif appointed Pervez Musharraf as the new Army Chief in October 1998 and soon after, directions were given to put the plan into effect.

To Nawaz Sharif, the success of this venture meant a great deal. It would make him a hero in the eyes of the Pakistanis and would add to his stature amongst Islamic fundamentalists. Pakistan badly needed a military success to bolster her sagging image after the 1971 Indo-Pakistan War and the Siachen stand-off. According to the Pakistani military hierarchy, the success of the venture was almost guaranteed.

Their logic was that the area was unheld, surprise would be total, and India was unlikely to react in a big way for fear of Pakistan's newly acquired nuclear deterrent. The plan offered attractive military opportunities, and the geo-political spin-offs were too big to ignore. The temptation for Nawaz Sharif therefore was probably too much for him to resist. Although he consistently professed ignorance, Pakistan's military hierarchy affirm that he had been briefed and the plan had received his support.

Soon after Musharraf took over as Chief of Army Staff in October 1998, action commenced for the build-up of weapons, ammunition, equipment and stores and for the training of troops in High Altitude Warfare.

The Line of Control from Manawar in Jammu to Gurez is tightly held by both sides and closely monitored by patrols, but in the area where the Kargil War was fought i.e., in the Mushkoh Valley, Dras, Kaksar and Batalik, there are huge 'unheld gaps' extending from 10 to 45 kilometres! So inaccessible and impassable is the ground configuration here, that both sides maintain posts only in summer, from which they launch patrols and withdraw them in winter, when heavy snowfall, avalanches and blizzards make survival in such difficult areas a formidable and impractical task. In any case, it is neither possible nor desirous to hold every inch of ground along the Line of Control. The important features are held and the gaps denied by patrolling and other means.

The Pakistani operation in Kargil was neither an encroachment nor an intrusion. It was in fact a well-planned offensive to capture and hold strategic areas as part of a bigger strategic plan. Their operations in Kargil took Indian military planners by surprise. In launching operations in Kargil, Pakistan breached the Simla Agreement and violated the sanctity of the Line of Control which had been maintained by both sides since 1972. India, however, has yet to learn from past experiences with Pakistan that Pakistan's credibility and conduct in these matters is at best highly questionable.

By early May 1999, Pakistan had extended her defences and operational and administrative support bases well across the Line of Control in the Mushkoh, Dras, Kaksar and Batalik Sectors. The extent of penetration across the Line of Control varied from 4 to 8 kilometres in each sector. Strong defensive positions were established by regular troops of the Northern Light Infantry and SSG (Special Service Group) commandos with full support of artillery, mortar, and anti-aircraft missiles and other heavy weapons. Military stores were dumped and extensive anti-personnel landmines laid. In all, a force approximately 2000 strong had transgressed into Indian territory. From the heights they commanded, the Srinagar-Leh highway was effectively interdicted. The first reports came in from local shepherds on 6 May 1999 and it took some time for the army to determine the size and extent of Pakistani ingress. A patrol that was sent out never returned and it was only on 10 June 1999 that the Pakistani Army returned the terribly mutilated bodies of the patrol leader and his five soldiers. The medieval bestiality of Pakistan's soldiers and the manner in which they treat prisoners of war shocked India and the world. What is inexplicable is that the Government of India besides making a few statements did not and has not to date taken it up more strongly with the International Court of Justice.

The amount of intrusion, when it was fully known was staggering. It became obvious to all that here was a major failure of intelligence, including military intelligence at all levels. The enemy had coolly come in, well within our territory, had established well fortified posts with all the necessary support and infrastructure and we did not know! It was clear to all, that the recapture of these posts situated on inaccessible features would be a very difficult operation. Fighting on mountains is always to the advantage of the defender, particularly in these sectors where hillsides are precipitous and steep, and covered with snow and ice. In this situation, the defender is secure behind his defences while the encumbered attacker is totally vulnerable in the open, as he negotiates and climbs steep slopes which at times are almost vertical and require the use of ropes. The defending Pakistani soldiers were very confident that they would beat back any attack by our soldiers, so great was their tactical advantage. They, however, did not reckon with one factor in the Indian armoury—'Courage'! Courage of the ill-equipped Indian infantryman whose bravery in battle must never be forgotten, and who was ably supported by the gunners who tried desperately to reduce the odds against their infantry brothers and the airforce pilots who wheeled far above their heads looking for opportunities to blast the defenders out of their complacency and their secure strongholds.

Courage in combat coloured the slopes of the Kargil battlefields crimson as soldiers shed their precious blood battling against superhuman odds. Attacks were launched at heights above 15,000 feet in sub-zero temperatures where every breath is painful at these rarified heights and every step a laboured effort. Encumbered with heavy backpacks they had to move agonisingly slow against withering automatic fire, showers of grenades and heavy enemy artillery and mortar fire. Added to this was the Government of India's decision not to cross the Line of Control thereby further reducing tactical options.

Conditions were nightmarish for battalion commanders when uncompromising orders from the top demanded results literally overnight. Yet these results were achieved but at a terrible cost. 25 officers and 436 jawans were killed at Kargil and 54 officers and 629 jawans were wounded, many of them disabled for life.

Nevertheless, no quarter was asked for and none given. Infantrymen attacked with a ferocity that astonished the Pakistani defenders; the gunners fired till their barrels were red hot; the pilots took great risks to blast the enemy strongholds and the supporting arms and services extended themselves well beyond their limits to provide the attacking soldiers the support they so badly needed and the media responded magnificently taking frontline battles into every Indian home, thereby activating tremendous public support that boosted the morale of the troops and encouraged them to even greater feats of daring.

The Pakistani government's lie that the intruders were Kashmiri freedom fighters was soon exposed with the capture of regular soldiers of the Pakistan Army. The recovery of bodies of Pakistani officers and soldiers of the Northern Light Infantry and large amounts of documents gave conclusive proof that the operation was launched by none else than the regular army of Pakistan.

Pakistani troops and the military hierarchy who were initially euphoric about their early success were taken aback by the determination and sagacity of the Indian political and military leadership and the courage and daring of her young officers and the soldiers they led. Slowly but steadily the enemy strongholds were systematically destroyed and the Pakistani defenders vanquished. Pakistan lost an estimated 45 officers and 700 soldiers and ultimately had nothing to show for it.

Meanwhile, the Indian Army deployed certain strategic forces to pre-empt any further Pakistani misadventure. The American media erroneously reported information from their spy-satellites that Indian desert forces were moving to their battle-locations. The Indian Navy as a precautionary move deployed its Western Fleet. These reports not only convinced the Pakistani leadership that India meant business but also so alarmed the Pakistani premier Nawaz Sharif, that he scuttled off to Washington to meet the American President to broker a ceasefire and to agree to pull back the so-called Mujahideen. But there was very little left to pull back because most of the battles had already been won and the areas recaptured. In fact, he must have received the news that Tiger Hill was recaptured by us even as he was preparing to meet the American President on 4 July 1999. The war in fact had already been won, and the so-called 'withdrawal' of the remaining forces was only a face-saving device to spare Pakistan any further humiliation.

It was in these daunting circumstances that four of the heroes of the Kargil War won their Param Vir Chakras. Two were officers and two were jawans, but only the two jawans lived to tell the tale.

Captain Vikram Batra
13 JAMMU AND KASHMIR RIFLES

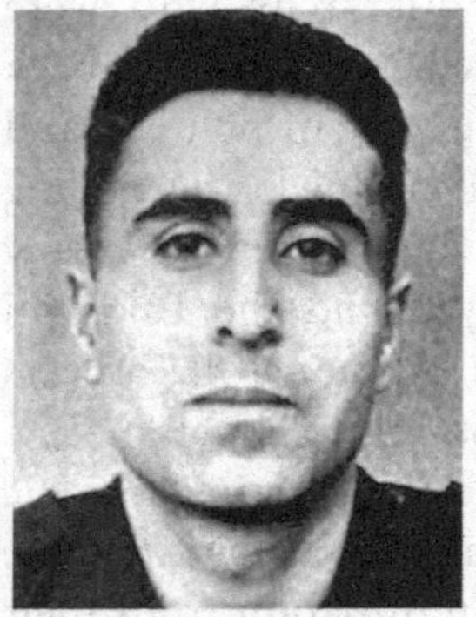

The Battles for the Capture of Hump, Pt 5140 and Pt 4875

13 Jammu and Kashmir Rifles was ordered to move to Dras on 12 June 1999 as reserve to 18 Grenadiers for the capture of a feature called 'Hump' which was in fact an extension of the Tololing feature. Hump along with Rocky Knob, another important feature in the vicinity was captured by 1700 hours on 17 June 1999 after two nights of intense fighting. The enemy suffered 8 killed and 9 wounded and left behind 3 UMGs (Universal Machine Guns) and large quantities of ammunition. These UMGs were thereafter used by our troops against the enemy.

Capture of Pt 5140

The next task given to 13 Jammu and Kashmir Rifles was the capture of Pt 5140. This was one of the most strategically located and important features in the Dras Valley. It was from here that the enemy brought down one of our helicopters with a Stinger missile, and thereafter no helicopter could fly in the vicinity. Its capture therefore assumed paramount importance.

The task of capturing Pt 5140 was given to 'B' and 'D' Companies of 13 Jammu and Kashmir Rifles. 'B' Company commanded by Captain S.S. Jamwal and 'D' Company commanded by Captain Vikram Batra moved at 0400 hours on 19 June 1999 and concentrated on the western slopes of Hump by 0630 hours, and lay 'doggo' there for the day.

During the day, both the company commanders were briefed in detail by their Commanding Officer, Lieutenant Colonel Y.K. Joshi and thereafter both carried out a detailed reconnaissance of the area. It was during the briefing that Captain Vikram Batra told his Commanding Officer that the success signal for his company would be '*Yeh Dil Mange More*' (Give me more) and Captain S.S. Jamwal chose the words 'Oh Yeah! Yeah! Yeah!' as his success signal for his company. After dark both companies commenced moving towards Pt 5140 under cover of artillery fire. The climb to the top of the feature, which was approximately 15,000 feet high, was very tough due to precipitous slopes and the rarified atmosphere. The troops had to halt every now and then to gather their breath. The enemy carried out very effective illumination of the area using artillery para flares, which further slowed down the speed of the companies. He also brought down very effective artillery fire on the assaulting troops causing casualties. The companies however continued to advance against all odds. The companies reached the vicinity of the feature at 0315 hours. The feature had a total of 7 bunkers, 2 bunkers on the top and 5 bunkers towards the East. 'B' Company under Captain S.S. Jamwal reached the

Captain Vikram Batra, PVC, (posthumous) on Pt 5140.

top first and assaulted from the left. Just short of the assault, the enemy at Pt 5140 came on the radio net of 13 Jammu and Kashmir Rifles and made an attempt to demotivate the assaulting troops by challenging 'Sher Shah' (Captain Vikram Batra) and threatening him and his men saying that none of them would go back alive. They however got a mouthful from Vikram and everybody else from the battalion who were on the radio net. Their weak attempt at psychological warfare, if indeed that was their aim, failed miserably.

Captain S.S. Jamwal's company captured its objective, and at 0335 hours, his success signal 'Oh Yeah! Yeah! Yeah!' was music to the Commanding Officer's ears. In the meanwhile, Captain Vikram Batra's company fired three rockets on the eastern bunkers before attacking them with Captain Vikram Batra in the lead. Six Pakistani soldiers were killed and the remainder fled. At 0435 hours Captain Vikram Batra's voice came over the air with the now famous success signal *Yeh Dil Mange More*. Large quantities of arms and ammunition were recovered indicating that the Pakistani troops holding Pt 5140 were approximately a platoon.

The capture of Pt 5140 turned the tide of the battle in the Dras sector. The enemy was badly shaken after this operation, which owed its success to surprise and stealth, the resilience of the troops and the initiative and courage of its leaders. After the capture of Pt 5140, helicopters could land at Tololing Top. 13 Jammu and Kashmir Rifles was thereafter deinducted from Dras Sector on 26 June 1999 and sent for operations in the Mushkoh Valley.

Capture of Pt 4875

Pt 4875 was a feature of strategic importance. This feature located in the Mushkoh Valley was dominating the National Highway 1A from Dras to Matayan. A stretch of 30–40 kilometres was under observation from this feature and effective artillery fire could be brought to bear on this stretch at will. It was imperative that this feature was captured by our troops and the enemy evicted. Helicopters could not land at the Dras helipad as it was a registered enemy target and they had to fly low, hugging the Pandrass Ridge. 13 Jammu and Kashmir Rifles was given the task of capturing Pt 4875. The battalions rest, refit, and recoup at Ghumri was cut down and it was inducted into the Mushkoh Valley on 30 June 1999, and placed under the command of 79 Mountain Brigade for the capture of Pt 4875. The entire induction was carried out under the hours of darkness, as the enemy was able to observe the movement from Pt 4875. The Commanding Officer Lieutenant Colonel Y.K. Joshi, along with 'A' Company commander, Major S. Vijay Bhaskar climbed to a vantage point on 1 July 1999 for the initial reconnaissance and formulation of the attack plan. Discussion of the plan took place at HQ 79 Mountain Brigade on 2 July 1999. General Officer Commanding 8 Mountain Division, Major General Mohinder Puri and Brigadier Kakkar Commander 79 Mountain Brigade and Lieutenant Colonel Y.K. Joshi, Commanding Officer 13 Jammu and Kashmir Rifles attended the discussion

The battalion was inducted to the firebase, approximately 1500 metres short of Pt 4875 in a defiladed area. Ammunition and heavy weapons were dumped using fighting porters from the battalion and 28 Rashtriya Rifles over 2 days on 2 and 3 July 1999.

On 4 July, 1999, during the day, the company commanders of 'A' and 'C' Companies, Major S.V. Bhaskar and Major Gurpreet Singh carried out their final recce and showed the objectives to their 'O' groups. Artillery fire from Bofor guns and multi-barrel launchers commenced at 1800 hours on 4 July 1999. The attacking companies started on their assault at 2030 hours. The night was pitch dark and the ground was rocky and difficult to negotiate. 200 metres short of the objective the companies came under heavy fire. The assaulting companies deployed their automatics at 0430 hours and commenced firing at the strong fortifications at the top of the feature. Both companies after initial success got stalled due to heavy fire from Pt 4875 Flat Top and were in imminent danger of being 'day-lighted'.

The enemy brought down very effective small-arms fire and sniper fire on both the companies and due to the very restricted approaches all movement was stalled. At approximately 1015 hours on 5 July, 1999 'C' Company commander spoke to the Commanding Officer and explained the predicament and the area from where the enemy was bringing effective fire on him. The Commanding Officer, Lieutenant Colonel Joshi at this juncture personally fired two FAGOT missiles from the fire base and neutralised the enemy that was interfering. These were direct hits and the enemy was seen fleeing from the bunker. 'C' Company immediately assaulted the position with two sections and by 1300 hours 5 July 1999 Pt 4875 was captured. 'A' and 'C' Companies linked up and consolidated their hold on the feature but the enemy continued to fire at the troops from a feature in depth.

At 2200 hours on 5 July 1999, heavy and accurate fire was brought to bear on the two companies from a Pakistani position North of Pt 4875. Early next morning at 0445 hours on 6 July 1999, 'C' Company reported that it was running out of ammunition because of the intensity of the firefight that was going on. 'B' Company, which was in reserve, quickly brought up the ammunition and the exchange of fire continued.

On the night of 6–7 July 1999, the opposing forces were so close that verbal exchanges took place between the troops intermingled with fierce fighting. It became obvious at this stage that something had to be done quickly to destroy this Pakistani post as otherwise the situation could deteriorate. At this juncture, the presence of the enemy was detected on a long and narrow ledge, running north from Pt 4875. The enemy was occupying the ledge in strength and his defences consisted of strong sangars echeloned one behind the other. 'D' company was tasked to exploit and clear the Pakistani intruders from the Ledge. On 7 July 1999, since the advance of the company was being held up due to enemy resistance from a sangar in close proximity, Captain Vikram Batra volunteered to lead a party to move up and observe the area ahead of Pt 4875 and to obtain a foothold on the Ledge. In spite of heavy fire from enemy automatics and grenade firing launchers, Captain Vikram Batra moved forward and closed on to the sangar firing incessantly with his AK-47. He reached the very narrow entrance of the sangar and taking the enemy totally by surprise killed 5 Pakistani soldiers. However he was heavily outnumbered and was shot in the chest from very close range and as he fell down he was also hit by grenade splinters. Captain Vikram Batra displayed dedication to duty beyond the call of duty and made the supreme sacrifice of his life but not before paving the way for his company to advance further to capture the Ledge which in turn enabled his battalion to consolidate its hold on Pt 4875 and to eliminate the domination of the National Highway from Dras to Matayan.

Captain Vikram Batra always leading from the front, and fully aware of the great danger of his mission, displayed unparalleled courage and determination in eliminating a Pakistani position at Ledge because he was aware of the importance of his task. His daring assault enabled the completion of the capture of Pt 4875 and this broke the will of the enemy. His courage and action were well beyond the call of duty and he continued to take risks ultimately making the supreme sacrifice in the finest traditions of the Indian Army.

* * *

Citation

Captain Vikram Batra
13 JAMMU AND KASHMIR RIFLES (IC 57556)

During 'Operation Vijay', on 20 June 1999, Captain Vikram Batra, Commander Delta Company was tasked to attack Point 5140. Captain Batra with his company skirted around the feature from the East and maintaining surprise reached within assaulting distance of the enemy. Captain Batra reorganised his column and motivated his men to physically assault the enemy positions. Leading from the front, he in a daredevil assault, pounced on the enemy and killed four of them in a hand-to-hand fight. On 7 July 1999, in another operation in the area of Pt 4875, his company was tasked to clear a narrow feature with sharp cuttings on either side and heavily fortified enemy defences that covered

President K.R. Narayanan presenting the Param Vir Chakra (posthumous) to the father of Captain Vikram Batra, 13 Jammu and Kashmir Rifles.

the only approach to it. For speedy operation, Captain Batra assaulted the enemy positions along a narrow ridge and engaged the enemy in a fierce hand-to-hand fight and killed five enemy soldiers at point blank range. Despite sustaining grave injuries, he crawled towards the enemy and hurled grenades clearing the position with utter disregard to his personal safety, leading from the front, he rallied his men and pressed on the attack and achieved a near impossible military task in the face of heavy enemy fire. The officer, however, succumbed to his injuries. Inspired by his daredevil act, his troops fell upon the enemy with vengeance, annihilated them and captured Point 4875.

Captain Vikram Batra, thus, displayed the most conspicuous personal bravery and leadership of the highest order in the face of the enemy and made the supreme sacrifice in the highest traditions of the Indian Army.

Gazette of India Notification
No. 16—Press/2000

Yeh Dil Mange More

"I will come back – either whole or wrapped in the nation's tricolour but I will return."

– *Vikram Batra. Kargil 1999*

The Kargil War was a war where young officers of the Army were in their 'element'. In no previous war had young officers dominated the scene as did these young gladiators in Kargil. Amongst them were some who deserved better and some whose deeds were not recorded at all and therefore not recognised.

However, from amongst them all, the one who captured the imagination of the public the most through the media, was young Vikram Batra. His bold courage and the daredevil risks he took in mission after mission filled the public with wonder and awe. He seemed to be invincible but every time he sallied forth to meet new challenges and dangers, people prayed for his safe return. His code-name 'Sher-Shah' soon became his nickname and even the enemy soldiers came to know of it, and addressed him as such when they shouted challenges at each other above the tumult of battle.

Soon after he had re-captured a strategic hilltop at Kargil, Vikram Batra was asked by a TV correspondent how he felt. The bearded young soldier, watched by millions of drawing-room viewers, had promptly said: *'Yeh Dil Mange More.'* Capt Batra died soon after, killing four intruders in a hand-to-hand battle, while storming Point 5140 and won a Param Vir Chakra for his bravery.

Capt Batra was one of the two December 1997 batch Indian Military Academy (IMA) graduates to be posthumously awarded the PVC for their gallantry in 'Operation Vijay' at Kargil. The second was Lt Manoj Kumar Pandey, also of the 1997 batch from IMA, who charged, wounded through a hail of bullets, and cleared bunker after bunker at Kargil till his injuries got the better of him.

Capt Batra and Lt Pandey lost their lives, but they left behind a legacy that has inspired many more young men to join the defence forces, especially the Army. In fact, the last course at the IMA that ended on December 9, 2000, saw the passing out of 803 Gentlemen Cadets—the largest number since Independence.

IMA Commandant Lt Gen Yuvraj Mehta admits, 'The young men's enthusiasm is reflected in the fact that there has been an 8 to 10 per cent increase in the number of cadets presently opting for infantry, the fighting wing of the Army.'

Responding to the renewed enthusiasm of young Indians, the IMA has introduced new features in their curriculum. These include: computerisation and simulation facilities.

But probably the most important addition is the inclusion of gallantry award winners as trainers.

R.P. Nailwal
21 January 2001, *Sunday Times*

His slogan *Yeh Dil Mange More* took on new patriotic meanings ranging from what the country demanded of its soldiers, the support the soldiers expected from the people and what young officers like Captain Vikram Batra demanded from life itself—bigger risks, tougher challenges—it came to mean that no sacrifice was too great for a soldier to make for his country. It was in fact a statement that however great the challenge, it would be met, and more!

Captain Vikram Batra must have been aware of the risks he was taking but like most young officers, he never considered the possibility of death. He lived for the day, and he lived it one day at a time but he lived it fully. In the last operation before the ceasefire, his battalion offensive was held up because of very stubborn enemy resistance from a position that was virtually unapproachable. The only approach was across a very narrow ledge which was under total domination by the enemy and the chances of survival were very poor. Yet he took the risk and led his troops in a final assault that captured the position but in the process he lost his life. His last letter home shows more concern for his parents than for himself. He tells them of the success of his previous operation and he asks his parents to pray for the success of his next action.

'Don't know when I'll be moving down again, but whenever I get a chance I will call you up. Do pray for the success of my next op. Take care. Love always. Your son Vicky.'

Rifleman Sanjay Kumar

13 JAMMU AND KASHMIR RIFLES

The Battle for Pt 4875 in the Mushkoh Valley

The battle for Pt 4875 has already been described in the account of Captain Vikram Batra. 13 Jammu and Kashmir Rifles was awarded two Param Vir Chakras for the same operation. This is the first time in the history of our Army that two individuals of the same battalion have been awarded the nation's highest award for courage in the same operation. Rifleman Sanjay Kumar was awarded the Param Vir Chakra for his action in the capture of Flat Top, a feature of Pt 4875, and Captain Vikram Batra for his action in the capture of Ledge also a feature north of Pt 4875, but part of the same feature.

In the operation for the capture of Flat Top on 4 July 1999, Rifleman Sanjay Kumar volunteered to be the leading scout of the attacking column. As the attack progressed, enemy automatic fire from one of the sangars posed a serious challenge, stalling its progress. Rifleman Sanjay Kumar realising the seriousness of the situation charged the enemy sangar and in the hand-to-hand struggle that followed killed three of the intruders and disregarding his injuries charged the second sangar. The enemy taken by surprise fled leaving behind an Universal Machine Gun (UMG). Rifleman Sanjay Kumar picked up the UMG and used it to kill more of the fleeing enemy. His bold and courageous action motivated his comrades who rushed the remaining sangars and cleared Flat Top of the enemy. Although bleeding profusely from his wounds he refused to be evacuated till Flat Top was cleared of all the enemy. His bold and courageous act, well beyond the call of duty earned for him and his unit the nation's highest award for courage in the face of the enemy.

* * *

Citation

Rifleman Sanjay Kumar,
13 JAMMU AND KASHMIR RIFLES (13760533)

Rifleman Sanjay Kumar volunteered to be the leading scout of the attacking column tasked to capture area Flat Top of Point 4875 in the Mushkoh Valley on 4 July 1999. During the attack when enemy automatic fire from one of the sangars posed stiff opposition and

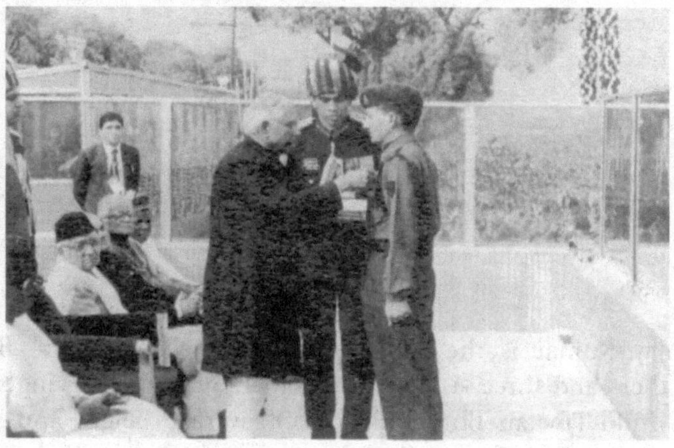

President K.R. Narayanan presenting the Param Vir Chakra to Rifleman Sanjay Kumar, 13 Jammu and Kashmir Rifles.

stalled the column, Rifleman Sanjay Kumar realising the gravity of the situation and with utter disregard to his personal safety, charged at the enemy. In the ensuing hand-to-hand combat, he killed three of the intruders and was himself seriously injured. Despite his injuries, he charged onto the second sangar. Taken totally by surprise, the enemy left behind a Universal Machine Gun and started running.

Rifleman Sanjay Kumar picked up the UMG and killed the fleeing enemy. Although bleeding profusely, he refused to be evacuated. The brave action on his part motivated his comrades and they took no notice of the treacherous terrain and charged onto the enemy and wrested the area Flat Top from the hands of the enemy.

Rifleman Sanjay Kumar displayed most conspicuous gallantry, cool courage and devotion to duty of an exceptionally high order in the face of the enemy.

Gazette of India Notification
No. 16—Press/2000

Against All Odds

The test of great love is not what it demands, but what it is prepared to do without.

– Anon

Sanjay Kumar is the youngest amongst six children—three brothers and three sisters. His brothers are both serving with the Indo-Tibetan Border Police. Of average height and slim in appearance, Sanjay is quiet and self-effacing by nature. He passed his 10th class from a neighbourhood school. His parents could not afford to educate him any further. Sanjay's uncle had served with the Jammu and Kashmir Rifles and was killed in the 1965 Indo-Pakistan War. Sanjay resolved to join the same regiment and went to the Branch Recruiting Office to be enrolled. He passed all the tests—written, physical, and medical but was not selected because of want of merit. He applied a second time, with the same result.

Frustrated and disappointed, Sanjay came to Delhi in search of a job. He learnt to drive jeeps and cars and returned to his hometown in Himachal Pradesh, and was employed as a taxi driver at Bilaspur. He was however still determined to join the Army and went to Jabalpur for recruitment. Third time proved lucky and he was enrolled in the Jammu and Kashmir Rifles. Sanjay was very happy to achieve his dream.

In 1999, Sanjay's battalion, 13 Jammu and Kashmir Rifles was stationed at Srinagar and was inducted into Dras in the first week of June 1999. On 4 July 1999 in the action at Flat Top and Ridge Sanjay exhibited extraordinary courage and bravery when he charged an enemy bunker through a hail of enemy bullets. Despite being hit twice in the chest and forearm and bleeding profusely from his wounds, he continued his charge and killed the enemy soldiers in the bunkers. Inspired by his action, his comrades assaulted the feature and captured it.

Sanjay's determination to join the army paid off, and his determination to do his duty in the face of certain death is an inspiration to us all.

Lieutenant Manoj Kumar Pandey
1/11 GORKHA RIFLES

Nothing is impossible. The difficult is done immediately.
The impossible may take a little more time.

– Indian Army

The Battle for Khalubar

The 1st Battalion the 11th Gorkha Rifles had just finished a tough assignment on the Siachen Glacier and the officers and men were looking forward to their peace tenure at Poona. The battalion advance party had already reached Poona and handed over its winter clothing, most of its weapons and equipment and a large number of its personnel had been sent on leave. The Commanding Officer had moved out on premature retirement, the second-in-command was on leave and the battalion was being commanded by the officiating second-in-command. Fighting a war at Siachen—the world's highest battlefield—has its own consequences. Climate and weather, besides the enemy, are implacable foes and the men were tired. Each man had lost about 5 kg in weight. It was in such a situation that the battalion, instead of proceeding to Poona, was ordered for operations in the Kargil Sector and told to move to Batalik.

Divested of its major equipment, very short on manpower and in the absence of its Commanding Officer the battalion was set impossible tasks. That it responded positively and achieved the impossible, speaks very highly of the calibre of its officers and the fortitude and resilience of its men.

When 1/11 Gorkha Rifles was launched on Operation Vijay, Lieutenant Manoj Pandey always volunteered for the toughest jobs. Predictably, he was the first officer to move to the forward posts. On 9 May 1999, it was he who recovered the dead bodies of four jawans of another unit who were part of a patrol ambushed by the Pakistanis in our own area. Soon after, it was his mission that established contact with Kukar Thang which led to its eventual capture. Yet again, he was part of the team that captured Jubar and it was he who established the first post there.

On 2–3 July 1999, 'B' Company 1/11 Gorkha Rifles was given the task of capturing Khalubar. Lieutenant Manoj Pandey who was No. 5 Platoon Commander led the advance to Khalubar and as it approached it came under heavy fire from the surrounding heights, including area 'Bunkers'. Lieutenant Manoj Pandey was assigned to clear the bunkers. He manoeuvred his platoon to a position of advantage and assigned Havildar Bhim Bahadur's Section to assault the two right bunkers while he himself proceeded to clear the four bunkers on the left. Fearlessly attacking them, one after another he managed to kill four of the enemy. He was, however, wounded in his shoulder and legs while attacking and clearing the third bunker. Undaunted and paying no heed to his wounds he led the assault on the fourth bunker, shouting the Gorkha war cry *Ayo Gorkhali* (The Gorkhas have arrived). It was while throwing a hand grenade at the fourth bunker that he received a Medium Machine Gun (MMG) burst on his forehead. The grenade however found its target and the occupants of the fourth bunker were annihilated but Lieutenant Manoj Pandey was himself killed.

As a result of his action, six strong enemy bunkers were captured with 11 Pakistani soldiers killed. A huge cache of arms and ammunition including one Air Defence Gun was captured. The capture of area 'Bunkers' now provided the vital firm base for the attacking companies which finally resulted in the fall of Khalubar. Lieutenant Manoj Pandey led his men from the front with courage, determination and spirit of self-sacrifice and despite his wounds inspired his men and set the tone for further acts of courage.

Citation

Lieutenant Manoj Kumar Pandey
1/11 GORKHA RIFLES (IC 56959)

Lieutenant Manoj Kumar Pandey took part in a series of boldly led attacks during 'Operation Vijay', forcing back the intruders with heavy losses in Batalik including the capture of Jaubar Top. On the night of 2/3 July 1999 during the advance to Khalubar as his platoon approached its final objective, it came under heavy and intense enemy fire from the surrounding heights. Lieutenant Pandey was tasked to clear the interfering enemy positions, to prevent his battalion from getting daylighted, being in a vulnerable position. He quickly moved his platoon to an advantageous position under

President K.R. Narayanan presenting the Param Vir Chakra (posthumous) to the father of Lieutenant Manoj Kumar Pandey, 1/11, Gorkha Rifles.

intense enemy fire, sent one section to clear the enemy positions from the right and himself proceeded to clear the enemy positions from the left. Fearlessly assaulting the first enemy position, he killed two enemy personnel and destroyed the second position by killing two more. He was injured on the shoulder and legs while clearing the third position. Undaunted and without caring for his grievous injuries, he continued to lead the assault on the fourth position urging his men and destroyed the same with a grenade, even as he got a fatal burst on his forehead. This singular daredevil act of Lieutenant Pandey provided the critical firm base for the companies which finally led to capture of Khalubar. The officer, however, succumbed to his injuries.

Lieutenant Manoj Kumar Pandey, thus, displayed most conspicuous bravery, indomitable courage, outstanding leadership and devotion to duty and made the supreme sacrifice in the highest traditions of the Indian Army.

Gazette of India Notification
No. 16—Press/2000

* * *

Gorkha Gladiator

"I am not afraid of death. In fact, if necessary – I will kill death."

– Manoj Pandey, before his last assault. Kargil 1999

Manoj Kumar Pandey, 'The Hero of Batalik' was born on 25 June 1975 at Lucknow to Gopi Chand and Mohini Pandey. Like many heroes of the past, Manoj was brought up on stories of valour and courage told by his mother and set on the path of moral uprightness by his father. Manoj not only absorbed these strong moral values but displayed grit and determination at a very young age.

Manoj, early in life, decided that he would like to be a military officer, leading his men into battle and doing great deeds for his country. He joined the Sainik School, Lucknow and then the National Defence Academy, Khadakvasla. Throughout his career as a student and as a cadet he was known for his intelligence and his honesty. He was not only a brilliant student but also a good sportsman.

Manoj was devoted to his family and was strongly influenced by his frail but brave mother and carried her brave message in his heart: 'Go forth my brave son and come back only in glory and honour.'

Manoj's dream came true when he was commissioned in the First Battalion, the 11th Gorkha Rifles and joined it in the Kashmir Valley. The very next day he took part in an important mission with his immediate senior, Second Lieutenant P.N. Datt, who made the ultimate sacrifice in an example of outstanding courage in anti-terrorist operations and won for himself and his unit the honour of the Ashok Chakra award, India's highest award for bravery in operations other than war.

Manoj, like the great heroes of the past, believed in pushing himself to the limit in the achievement of his objectives. Even though he had so little service, his focus always was service to his country without counting the cost. There are many incidents that prove the degree of his commitment, an essential part of his character. Soon after he joined the Army, young Manoj had taken out a patrol but its return was abnormally delayed causing concern. When it finally returned, two days later than scheduled, his Commanding Officer asked him the cause of his delay. His answer was typical. 'We were not able to get any militants, so we went further and further till we got them.' When the battalion was about to be inducted into Siachen, Manoj was doing the Young Officer's course.

Impatient and upset that he was not with his men when they were about to embark on a difficult assignment, Manoj wrote to his Commanding Officer to keep 'Bana Post' for him if the battalion went to the Northern Glacier and 'Pahalwan Post' if it went to the Central Glacier. These are the highest posts on the northern and central parts of the glacier and the most difficult assignments. Eventually, it was he who spent the longest tenure at 'Pahalwan', at a height of 19,700 feet. So energetic and enthusiastic was Manoj in the execution of his duties that his Commanding Officer used to say that 'Anchors were required to restrain young Manoj.' The toughest jobs were taken up by him, as everyone knew he would do them with a smile and it would be a job well done.

In Kargil he took part in every operation launched by the battalion and contributed largely to their success culminating in the capture of Khalubar where he made the ultimate sacrifice.

Manoj has left behind a legacy that the nation he loved so much can be proud of, one that will inspire future generations of young officers and jawans to follow. These words may perhaps catch the essence of his spirit.

> *Weapons cannot cleave him*
> *Nor fire burn him,*
> *Water cannot wet him,*
> *Nor wind dry him away.*

> — Bhagavad Gita

Pied Piper of Batalik

THE memory of the Pied Piper haunts me. A young officer, full of life, dancing ahead of the children. The village children, wild with joy, running after him. The piper would suddenly stop, turn around and shower sweets. The children would catch them and then again sprint after the piper. The piper of Tamisgamn, as we would later call him.

After humouring the kids, he came to the platform and won the respect of the world village with his humble words. On the mike, with the whole village in the backdrop, standing tall . . . that's how our camera caught him. Now those photographs my children hold next to their hearts as they narrate stories of Pandey Uncle, their Pied Piper who became the target of enemy bullets and is known to the country as the Batalik hero, Captain Manoj Pandey.

In the spring of March 1999, that's when we met you, on our visit to Leh. In those evenings in the mess while we played dumb charades and other games in the dim lights of the overworked generator, your presence of mind and sense of humour never failed to amuse us. In the afternoons children would wait for your return for a pre-lunch session of darts and table tennis. The picnics and outings arranged by you and other young unit officers are etched in our minds as the most memorable and happiest times in our lives.

The virgin land of Ladakh beginning to bloom in spring, the majestic Himalayas silently being cut through by the Indus and serene monasteries were a perfect picture. This heavenly abode was the best place for the infantry battalion to unwind after a tough and successful tenure at the glacier. At dinner time after a drink or two sometimes we would hear the tales of the glacier, tales which were frightening and hair-raising, tales of brave adventure, rough climate, tough terrain. Tales of hidden crevasses and steep climbs, of sickness and laughter. Tales which a husband would never tell his wife or a son his mother. Listening to all these, admiration and respect for each one of you was strengthened. Silently, we would thank the Almighty for His blessing.

Innocently we thought it was all over. We laughed and planned for the unit's move. Little did we know that there was a tougher test left for each of you and these happy moments would be short-lived. In those few days we all had fun and good times not knowing that they would be the last few precious memories of you. Henceforth we all cherish them along with tales of your bravery. Most vividly we remember the welfare mela you organised single-handedly. I remember the discussion and planning that went into it, the minute details taken care of by you. The entire village was somehow involved. Small children performing their traditional dance; and for the hungry there were fancy eats. You had thought of them all. The mela was a great success.

On our way back, one of us mentioned that it was the first of April the next day, so let's have a little fun. Somehow you became the target. A plot was hatched and at dinner time you received a signal to report immediately at Mhow for a mortar course. You were tired after a long day and for a few minutes totally confused as to how to manage it all. Suggestions were innumerable. We controlled our laughter and wished you luck. The whole night you pretended to pack and prepare for your departure the next morning. The other young officers danced to bid you farewell. In the morning you loaded your empty bags, said your goodbyes and got into the vehicle. At the gate was a notice saying 'April Fool's Day' and you were told to get back. On your return, there was laughter and the biggest question was who made a fool of whom. Such were the feelings and joy we all shared. But now in your martyrdom you have left us all behind. You have reached great heights and memories are all that we have of you. The brave Gorkha officer, we all salute you.

Shobita Asthana
Indian Express, 10 September 1999

Grenadier Yogender Singh Yadav
18 GRENADIERS

The Battle for Tiger Hill

The Tiger Hill complex is one of the most dominating and awe-inspiring features in the Dras Sector. Pakistani soldiers had occupied this in strength and were bringing effective artillery fire on large tracts of the National Highway 1A. Eviction of the enemy from this feature was urgent and important. It was the key to enemy positions in the Dras Sector. The Tiger Hill complex was isolated from the north, south and east by 8 Sikh on 21 May 1999. However, isolation from the west could not be done as the complete ridge line was occupied by the enemy. The Indian Army moreover was not permitted to cross the Line of Control to get behind the enemy to cut his line of communications.

On the night of 3–4 July 18 Grenadiers was assigned the task of capturing Tiger Hill from the east with 8 Sikh providing the firm base. 8 Sikh was also tasked to simulate attacks from the south and north as also to cut off Tiger Hill from the west.

The attack on Tiger Hill commenced on 3 July at 2030 hours. By 0130 hours 4 July, 18 Grenadiers had captured part of its objective and 8 Sikh, exploiting the success of its simulated attacks, also captured important features of Tiger Hill on its western spur by 0400 hours, 5 July 1999, thereby isolating the enemy deployed on Tiger Hill.

Meanwhile 18 Grenadiers continued attacking its remaining objectives on Tiger Hill and capturing them against fierce opposition. Counter-attacks against objectives captured by 8

Sikh were repulsed and beaten back. The final objectives of Tiger Hill were captured by 18 Grenadiers on 11 July 1999 and the battle of Tiger Hill was over.

The determination, raw courage, grit and determination displayed by all ranks of 18 Grenadiers and 8 Sikh was exemplary and worthy of emulation.

During the first phase of the attack on the night of 3–4 July 1999 Grenadier Yadav's Ghatak (Commando) Platoon was tasked to capture 'Three Bunkers'. The approach to this was a vertical cliff face, snowbound and at a height of 16,500 feet. Grenadier Yogender Singh Yadav volunteered to lead the assault and climbed the rock face fixing the ropes for further assault on the feature. On reaching half-way up, an enemy bunker opened up with machine-gun and rocket fire killing his platoon commander and two of his comrades. Realising the critical situation Yogender continued to scale the sheer cliff-face alone through the heavy volume of fire. In spite of having been hit by three bullets in his groin and shoulder, displaying superhuman strength and resolve, he climbed the remaining 60 feet all by himself and reached the top, crawled upto the enemy bunker and lobbed grenades that killed all four of its occupants. Disregarding his injuries Grenadier Yadav charged the second bunker with two of his colleagues who had joined him by now and killed three Pakistani soldiers in a fierce hand-to-hand combat.

His extraordinary and courageous action so inspired the rest of his platoon that it charged the remainder of the Pakistani position on Tiger Hill which helped greatly towards its capture after some more fighting.

* * *

Citation

Grenadier Yogender Singh Yadav
18 GRENADIERS (2690572)

Grenadier Yogender Singh Yadav was part of the leading team of a Ghatak Platoon tasked to capture Tiger Hill on the night of 3/4 July 1999. The approach to the top was steep, snowbound and rocky. Grenadier Yogender Singh Yadav, unmindful of the danger involved, volunteered to being the lead and fixed the rope for his team to climb up. On seeing the team, the enemy opened intense automatic, grenade, rocket and artillery fire killing the Commander and two of his colleagues and the platoon was stalled. Realising the gravity of the situation, Grenadier Singh Yadav crawled up to the enemy position to silence it and in the process sustained multiple bullet injuries. Unmindful of his injuries and

President K.R. Narayanan presenting the Param Vir Chakra to Havildar Yogender Singh Yadav, 18 Grenadiers.

in the hail of enemy bullets, Grenadier Yogender Yadav continued climbing towards the enemy positions, lobbed grenades, continued firing from his weapons and killed four enemy soldiers in close combat and silenced the automatic fire. Despite multiple bullet injuries, he refused to be evacuated and continued the charge. Inspired by his gallant act, the platoon charged on to the other positions with renewed punch and captured Tiger Hill Top.

Grenadier Yogender Singh Yadav displayed the most conspicuous courage, indomitable gallantry, grit and determination under extreme adverse circumstances.

Gazette of India Notification
No. 16—Press/2000

* * *

The Last Ghatak

'Love's nobility is shown in this, that it strengthens us to make sacrifices for others . . . '

– James Russel Lovell

Yogender Singh Yadav was born on 10 May 1980 at the village of Aurangabad Ahir, Bulandshar, UP, approximately 50 kilometres east of Meerut. At the time he was awarded the Param Vir Chakra, he was just 19 years old.

Yogender's father, Karan Singh Yadav is an ex-serviceman of the Kumaon Regiment and had taken part in the 1965 and 1971 Indo-Pakistan Wars. As a young boy, Yogender and his brothers would listen to their father's battle experiences, and the two elder boys decided that they too would join the Army. The elder brother Sepoy Jitender Singh Yadav, was recruited into the Artillery. Yogender followed and was recruited by the Grenadier Regiment at the age of 16 years 5 months.

As far as he can remember, Yogender has been deeply impressed by the lives of persons who have made great sacrifices for the nation: Sardar Bhagat Singh who went to his death with a smile having struck a decisive blow for India's freedom; Subhas Chandra Bose who at a comparatively young age raised an army to free India from foreign domination; Rani Lakshmi Bai of Jhansi who as a young woman died fighting the British. The concept of fighting for a great cause, like liberating one's country from domination or against an invading enemy stirred him greatly and he recounts that each time he read these stories his hair would stand on end. The life of Babar also impressed him because he was able to achieve so much at such a young age having established his kingdom in India at the age of sixteen. Doing what they did in the prime of their lives influenced him very much and he often wondered whether one day he too would be able to emulate the deeds of his heroes.

That day came sooner than expected. Yogender Singh Yadav is the youngest recipient of the Param Vir Chakra—India's highest award for valour.

Conclusion of the War in Kargil

An army is of little value in the field unless there are wise counsels at home.

— Marcus Tullius Cicero

Kargil is a war that should never have happened. It proved that 'the only lesson we learn from history is that we do not learn from history.' The war in Kargil is a combination of most of our mistakes of the past. Will there be more Kargils? Undoubtedly yes, unless the political and military hierarchy are able to accept that there were major shortcomings in our systems that allowed Pakistan to attempt this foolish venture, and also to ensure that these will never again be repeated. Questions that the civil and military hierarchy needs to answer are—does it accept the need to elicit and accept feedback, does it have the ability to demand and obtain for the armed forces the weapons and equipment that they need for fighting a war, and does it have the capacity to accept and ensure responsibility and accountability up and down the chain of command? The failure of intelligence both civil and military, endemic since Independence, will continue to be our Achilles heel until the powers that be accept this deficiency and take steps to set this right.

That we were caught flat-footed in an area of accepted vulnerability is inexcusable and that primarily includes the troops and commanders on the ground. What was worse was the tendency to pass the buck and to initially push troops to rectify the situation without ensuring the basic requisites to accomplish near-impossible tasks.

After the event, the government appointed a committee which came to be known as the Kargil Review Committee. It was asked 'to review events that led to the Pakistani aggression in Kargil and to recommend such measures considered necessary to safeguard national security against such armed intrusion'. The report is rich in military history, military geography and details about 'what happened', but is blissfully blank about responsibility and accountability. When questioned about this aspect, the Committee's answer that this was not part of its charter failed to impress listeners. One would like to ask the committee whether 'responsibility and accountability' are not preliminary to 'measures considered necessary to safeguard national security'? The inability of the government to handle the aspect of accountability has given the impression that the report conceals more than it reveals, and unless we have more transparency in our systems we are likely to have similar situations arising again. And that is sad.

Having said this, it needs also to be said that the government and the armed forces clearly demonstrated the 'will to win' once the situation became clear, and exhibited skills in the diplomatic and military fields that were reassuring and commendable. Despite tremendous political, economic and diplomatic pressures it exhibited clear vision, an unambiguous aim, firm purpose, and unequivocal determination to remove the intrusion. Their decisions received the whole-hearted cooperation of the ground and air forces and the young officers who led from the front.

The four Param Vir Chakras are a sample of bravery of the highest kind and there are many more stories of outstanding courage that need to be told. Hopefully someone will write about them someday.

CHAPTER VI

UN PEACEKEEPING OPERATIONS AND THE WAR AT SIACHEN

UN Peacekeeping
Operations and the War at Siachen

∎

India was a member of the League of Nations and subsequently become a founder member of the United Nations Organisation (UNO) on 24 October 1945. One of the major aims of the UN is to ensure world peace. Despite the mandate that the UN gave itself there have been a number of wars and conflicts that have taken place in different parts of the world and which continue to occur. While the UN may not have been able to prevent all such conflicts, it has certainly helped in keeping them within limits and from growing into bigger wars. It has also helped in bringing about a cessation of hostilities, and in many cases helped to bring about a resolution of such situations.

Indian national policy has also been oriented to world peace and it has therefore been a staunch supporter of the UN in her mission of conflict resolution between warring nations in different parts of the world. In the last fifty-five years since Independence, India has participated in 31 of the United Nations peacekeeping operations in which over 35,000 Indian soldiers have taken part. Some of these have been difficult operations and our troops have suffered casualties in their efforts to ensure peace. So far 93 officers and men of the armed forces have made the supreme sacrifice on the altar of world peace.

Most prominent amongst those who gave up their lives in the cause of peace is Captain Gurbachan Singh Salaria who was awarded the Param Vir Chakra, India's highest award for outstanding courage and valour displayed in the face of armed rebels in the Congo.

India today is ranked as the second largest troop contributor for UN peacekeeping missions. In this, it has demonstrated professional competence of a very high order and also its ability to sustain large troop commitments over prolonged periods.

In UN peacekeeping operations, military personnel are required to keep the peace not by force of arms but by mature and balanced behaviour, correct attitude, a high sense of discipline and responsibility and respect for human life and dignity. A soldier is therefore called upon to use his professional competence in a stable and diplomatic manner and to act impartially in the establishment of peace. This requires a high degree of motivation and training and the Indian soldier has demonstrated an outstanding ability to learn and to apply these techniques and behaviour skills. The Indian Army also follows an uncompromising system of selection to pick the best contingents of officers and men for such UN assignments.

In some instances as the high casualty list would indicate, Indian troops have had to fight in order to implement the UN mandate. These operations which unfortunately, have been on the increase in recent times, have come to be known as peace-enforcement operations—undesirable but unavoidable. At times, the UN has had to itself form a UN Force to counter aggression. The UN operation in the Congo was one such operation.

UN Operations in the Belgian Congo 1960
Captain Gurbachan Singh Salaria

3/1 GORKHA RIFLES

The Belgian Congo unlike the colonies of the British, French and the Dutch, was only conceded independence by Belgium on 30 June 1960 after a bloody struggle. The people of the colony were kept extremely backward. Foreign commercial interests as well as Belgium itself continued to exploit them even after independence. Congo had many teething problems. First, the army mutinied. Subsequently Belgium intervened without concurrence of the Congolese government; later, one of the provinces, Katanga seceded, followed by another province, Kasai. European interests could be seen behind all these. Congo appealed to the UN for help and this was promptly sanctioned on 14 July 1960. Belgium was called upon to withdraw its forces and it was decided to despatch UN troops to restore normalcy and to provide economic assistance. India initially provided some logistic support to the UN command and subsequently provided a brigade on request from the UN. 99 Infantry Brigade Group, under Brigadier K.A.S. Raja, was sent by air and sea to Leopoldville, the capital, between March and June 1961. Moise Kapenda Tshombe the leader of the breakaway Katanga province had a gendarmerie comprising thousands of troops under Belgian Officers. The UN command initially tried to effect a reconciliation between the breakaway provinces and the Central Government, but could not succeed. It was, therefore, decided to use force to bring the provinces back into the country. 99 Infantry Brigade, less a battalion, was sent to Katanga province for the purpose. It was initially located in the area of Albertville and cleared Northern Katanga by July 1961. It was thereafter moved to Elizabethville and operations were mounted to gain control of the rest of Katanga. This also succeeded. Moise Kapenda Tshombe however escaped to Northern Rhodesia. Subsequently, in September, a ceasefire was effected but the gendarmerie again started hostilities in November. Indian troops once again had to deal firmly with the situation. In these operations Captain Gurbachan Singh Salaria of 3/1 Gorkha Rifles was awarded the Param Vir Chakra, posthumously, for valour of the most exceptional order.

The Action at the Roadblock at Elizabethville

On 24 November 1961 the Security Council of the UN passed a resolution for UN forces to take vigorous action, including the use of force to immediately apprehend and detain all foreigners including mercenaries not under UN command. This brought out a violent reaction from Tshombe and his mercenaries. Two senior UN officers were taken captive, beaten and later released. Major Ajit Singh of 3/1 Gorkha Rifles was also taken captive and his driver brutally murdered. Plans were underway by the foreign mercenary officers to isolate the UN detachments around Elizabethville by the erection of roadblocks thus preventing intercommunication between the UN detachments to enable the mercenaries to eliminate the UN force detachments one by one. It was apparent by this time that Kimba, Minister of Foreign Affairs, had no control over the gendarmerie and that foreign mercenaries were fully in control.

On 5 December, roadblocks were hampering the movement of UN forces in and around Elizabethville. Around 0900 hours on 5 December 1961, 3/1 Gorkha Rifles received orders to clear the roadblock which was near the airport and the area called 'roundabout'. It was being held by approximately 150 gendarmes with two armoured cars.

The plan for clearing the airport roadblock in the area 'roundabout' was a simple one. Charlie Company 3/1 Gorkha Rifles under Major Govind Sharma was to attack the roadblock with a troop of Irish armoured personnel carriers. Captain Gurbachan Singh Salaria with a platoon of 'A' Company supported by a troop of Swedish armoured personnel carriers was to close in from the airport side and block the gendarmerie's route of withdrawal and to attack from that direction if so required. The remainder of 'A' company was to be in reserve. Midday was fixed as the time for the attack—a time the gendarmerie least expected.

Captain Gurbachan Singh Salaria managed to reach the specified location with his troops and the armoured personnel carriers. His rocket launcher team, making good use of ground, managed to get close to the enemy's armoured cars and to destroy both of them. Captain Gurbachan Singh Salaria felt that this was the best time to evict the gendarmerie before it had time to reorganise, and that any further delay would be detrimental to his mission. Fully realising the disproportionate ratio of force of his small platoon of 16 men and himself against more than 100 of the enemy, he rallied his men behind him and charged the enemy position in a khukri assault. More than 40 of the enemy were killed but Captain Gurbachan Singh Salaria was shot at by a gendarme sergeant. Two bullets pierced his neck and he collapsed on the last line of trenches. The ferocity of the attack, the blood curdling war cry of the Gorkhas *Ayo Gorkhali* (the Gorkhas have arrived) and the flashing khukris was too much for the gendarmerie which fled in confusion leaving its dead and wounded behind. Captain Gurbachan Singh Salaria however did not survive his injuries. His personal courage in the face of the enemy, his utter disregard for his own safety, and his unflinching devotion to duty earned him the posthumous award of the Param Vir Chakra.

* * *

Citation

Captain Gurbachan Singh Salaria
3/1 GORKHA RIFLES (IC-8947)

On 5 December 1961, 3/1 Gorkha Rifles was ordered to clear a roadblock established by the gendarmerie at a strategic roundabout at Elizabethville, Katanga. The plan was that one company with 2 Swedish armoured cars would attack the position frontally and Captain Gurbachan Singh Salaria with two sections of Gorkhas and two Swedish armoured personnel carriers would advance towards this roadblock from the airfield to act as a cutting-off force.

Captain Salaria with his small force arrived at a distance of 1500 yards from the roadblock at approximately 1312 hours on 5 December 1961 and came under heavy automatic and small-arms fire from an undetected enemy position dug in on his right flank. The enemy also had two armoured cars and about 90 men opposing Captain Salaria's small force.

Captain Salaria appreciating that he had run into a subsidiary roadblock and ambush and that this enemy force might reinforce the strategic roundabout and thus jeopardise the main operation, decided to remove this opposition. He led a charge with bayonets, khukris, and grenades supported by a rocket launcher. In this gallant engagement, Captain Salaria killed 40 of the enemy and knocked out the two armoured cars. This unexpected bold action completely demoralised the enemy who fled despite their numerical superiority and protected positions.

Captain Salaria was wounded in his neck by a burst of automatic fire but continued to fight till he collapsed due to profuse bleeding. Captain Salaria's gallant action prevented any enemy movement of the enemy force towards the main battle scene and thus contributed very largely to the success of the main battalion's action at the roundabout and prevented the encirclement of UN Headquarters in Elizabethville. Captain Salaria subsequently died of his wounds.

Captain Salaria's personal example, utter disregard for personal safety and dauntless leadership inspired his small but gallant force of sixteen Gorkhas to hold on to their position, dominate the enemy and to inflict heavy casualties despite the enemy's superiority in numbers and tactical position.

Captain Gurbachan Singh Salaria's leadership, courage, unflinching devotion to duty and disregard for personal safety were in the best traditions of our Army.

Gazette of India Notification
No. 8—Press/62

* * *

From Boy to Man to Martyr

Courage is the first of human qualities because it guarantees all the others.

— *Winston Churchill*

Gurbachan Singh Salaria was born on 29 November 1935 in village Janwal, near Shakargarh (now part of Pakistan). His father had already been drafted into the British Indian Army many years earlier in the Dogra squadron of Hodson's Horse. His mother Dhan Devi, was bold and courageous and her main focus was the well-being of her family and the education of her children. Gurbachan was their second child. He inherited his mother's courage and determination. Listening to the heroic tales and deeds of his father and his cavalry regiment Gurbachan from the very beginning had decided to join the Army.

His grandfather, a prosperous farmer was the lambardar (headman of the village) of the village, but the family had to move to India at the time of Partition and settled in village Jangal near Dinanagar in Gurdaspur district. Gurbachan joined the village school. He was good at his studies but better still at games which was to stand him in good stead when he joined King George's Royal Military College, (known today as King George's Rashtriya Military College) Bangalore in 1946 at the age of eleven. In August 1947, Gurbachan was transferred closer home to KGRMC Jallandar. He would never return to his village Janwal. These were difficult times for the Salaria family because the new areas were totally underdeveloped and the family had to start all over again from scratch. But his parents' determination and sense of sacrifice saw them through.

Gurbachan was somewhat quiet and reserved. He also had a sense of dignity, and righteousness. He was friendly, but his friends were restricted. He was straightforward, upright and simple in his habits. Self-respect meant a lot to him and he was intolerant of injustice and abuse of power. An incident that occurred at the KGRMC is indicative. One day the school bully roughed him and his friend up. Gurbachan challenged him to a boxing bout in the ring and although his opponent was much bigger and tougher than him, Gurbachan fought with such ferocity that he beat him up and knocked him out. He also made him promise that he would not bully anyone else in future. In another incident, he had to be restrained from jumping into a well to save a boy in distress when he did not even know how to swim.

In 1953 he joined the Joint Services Wing of the National Defence Academy. He was average at studies but an excellent sportsman, especially in boxing and water-polo. In 1956 he graduated to the Indian Military Academy and passed out on 9 June 1957 as a corporal. His love for the Gorkhas originated at Dehra Dun—their simplicity, professional competence, reputation for bravery and courage, their loyalty and sense of discipline and justice matched his own character traits and he and his close friend Sohan Nathani both opted for and got Gorkha regiments. Gurbachan was commissioned into 2/3 Gorkha Rifles and in March 1960 was transferred to 3/1 Gorkha Rifles.

Gurbachan also had an overwhelming determination to win—but by fair means. Also important to him were duty, responsibility and courage, both physical and moral. He was unmindful of consequences. The right thing had to be done and done immediately. It was perhaps these character traits that motivated him to attack and remove an enemy position nearly ten times his strength. He succeeded beyond measure but ultimately paid the price with his own life.

Operation Pawan 1987–1990

The problem in Sri Lanka between the Sinhalese and the Tamil minority had been festering for a long time. The Tamil minority which constitutes approximately 18 per cent of the population felt that their interests were neglected. Although the Sinhalese comprise the overwhelming majority, they form only 15 per cent of the population in the Northern and Eastern Provinces. Having failed to safeguard their rights by peaceful means, the Tamils felt compelled to take to arms and declared their intention to achieve Tamil Eelam—a separate state for the Tamils. In doing this, they chose to disregard the experience of India and Pakistan, their northern neighbours, where the 1947 Partition caused two million dead when the country was divided on the basis of racial majority areas.

The Sri Lankan government tried to put down the Tamil movement by force but failed and this resulted in the Tamils taking to guerrilla warfare. The resulting disturbances caused a large number of refugees emigrating to the southern Indian state of Tamil Nadu. This in turn created considerable problems for India. The situation was reminiscent of the situation in East Pakistan in 1971. The birth of Bangladesh with India's assistance perhaps fired the Tamils' dream of the establishment of a Tamil Eelam with India's help. There were, however, many differences in the two situations, the major one being that the Tamils were a minority and not the majority citizens of the state. However, after protracted negotiations, in which leaders of various Tamil groups were involved, an agreement was arrived at between Sri Lanka and India on 29 July 1987.

In accordance with the agreement, an Indian Peace Keeping Force (IPKF) was inducted into Sri Lanka on 3 August 1987. Arms were to be surrendered by the militant groups to the IPKF after which various other measures were to be taken, including elections with a view to giving Tamils considerable autonomy. The IPKF was to assist in establishing peace and ensuring normalcy. Fighting to enforce peace was never envisaged. Whilst most of the militant groups laid down their arms, the Liberation Tigers of Tamil Eelam (LTTE) surrendered only a few of their weapons. Further, following an incident in which some LTTE personnel committed suicide by swallowing cyanide capsules on 5 October 1987 while in Sri Lankan custody, the LTTE resumed violence. The IPKF instead of being the peacekeeping force now became the target of LTTE violence.

The IPKF which consisted at that time of only 54 Infantry Division, went into action in the Jaffna area (Northern Province) on 10 October 1987 to clear the area of hostile forces and secure their surrender. It took about three weeks to clean the area at the cost of heavy casualties due to ambushes, mines, and booby traps. The LTTE subsequently commenced guerrilla operations in the Eastern Province and it became apparent that many more troops were required to establish control. Over a period of time, three more divisions—4, 36, and 57 were inducted into Sri Lanka to deal with the LTTE.

It soon became apparent however that the task which now began to devolve on the IPKF had changed beyond imagination. The original task was quite different from what was now required. Troops that were inducted into Sri Lanka were neither trained nor equipped for the tasks they now faced. Even basic requirements like maps were not available to them. They lacked proper logistic support, had no intelligence whatsoever, and most important, the political aim was uncertain, wavering and infirm. Troops were inducted into the theatre piecemeal, untrained, improperly equipped and without proper logistics. The fighting command had too many masters each making different assessments and giving different orders. The Prime Minister, Chief of the Army Staff, the Vice Chief of Army Staff, General Officer Commanding-in-Charge Southern Command, Director of Military Operations, the High Commission in Colombo were all involved in a tangled command web that did not make it easy for the Force Commander to carry out his task.

The troops on the ground were also aware that whereas they were operating against Tamil insurgents, the insurgents were being trained in India by other agencies, were being supplied with large quantities of arms and equipment money, and moral support from Tamil Nadu. This had a very adverse effect on the morale of the troops. Worst of all, the troops on the ground were not able to distinguish friend from foe. The LTTE not only operated in civilian clothes but also used civilian women and children as human shields behind which they targeted our troops making it nearly impossible for them to retaliate.

In was in this tangled web of political and military contradictions that the IPKF and officers of the Indian Army like Major Ramaswamy Parameswaran had to operate.

The Action at Kantarodai

Major Ramaswamy Parameswaran's battalion, 8 Mahar, took part in Operation Pawan as part of 91 Infantry Brigade and 54 Infantry Division. It was inducted into the Jaffna Peninsula in Sri Lanka on 30 July 1987, a day after the 'Indo-Sri Lanka Peace Accord' was signed. The battalion was the first unit of the Indian Army to have landed in Sri Lanka as part of the IPKF (Indian Peace Keeping Force). During its tenure in Sri Lanka, the battalion undertook a number of operations against the LTTE, the major ones being at Maruthanamadam, Annai Kotai, Manipai and Kantarodai. It was at Kantarodai that Major Ramaswamy Parameswaran fought his gallant action which is the focus of our attention.

On 24 November 1987, the battalion received information that a consignment of arms and ammunition had been unloaded at a house in the village of Kantarodai. A strong patrol of 20 men was sent under command of Captain D.R. Sharma to check the veracity of this information. The patrol was fired upon from the vicinity of a temple near the suspected house and after an exchange of fire the patrol sent information to the battalion at Uduvil that the area was under occupation of the LTTE, and that their strength was more than was estimated.

Major Ramaswamy Parameswaran, Company Commander 'A' Company came to the conclusion that a proper operation would have to be launched and taking a strong patrol from his company proceeded at 2030 hours to reinforce Captain Sharma's patrol. Both patrols now joined together and proceeded towards the suspected house.

Major Ramaswamy Parameswaran's company reached the vicinity of the suspects' house around 0130 hours on 25 November 1987. They saw no movement except for an empty truck parked near the house. They cordoned off the area and decided to carry out a search after first light.

The search commenced at 0530 hours on 25 November 1987 but found nothing. They finally decided to move back. At this time the point section drew fire from the temple-grove area which was effective and pinned it down. The party went to ground and returned the fire. The first burst of enemy fire resulted in one dead and one wounded. Major Ramaswamy Parameswaran briefed Captain D.R. Sharma to keep the enemy occupied and fixed by returning effective fire from the same place and to simultaneously advance by clearing the route house by house, while he and his party took a detour from the west to go behind the LTTE and to trap them in the temple-grove area.

When Captain D.R. Sharma started moving forward he drew heavy automatic fire from the areas of the temple grove and coconut grove. Captain D. R. Sharma's party cleared the houses on the west of the road and saw some dead and wounded militants being dragged away by their colleagues. In the meantime Major Ramaswamy Parameswaran had reached behind the militants in the area of the coconut grove and seeing the enemy he charged at them. During the ensuing hand-to-hand fight, one of the militants shot him in the chest. Undaunted and unmindful of his grave injury, he snatched the rifle from the militant and shot him dead. Now, notwithstanding his condition he continued to give directions to his troops and to inspire them till he collapsed. The militants who by now sensed that they had been trapped fought their way back and in the ensuing fighting both sides suffered casualties.

In the meanwhile, Captain D.R. Sharma had cleared the houses adjoining the area of the coconut grove and moved towards the temple grove. Reinforcements from the battalion had also arrived. The militants realising that they would be defeated melted away into the jungle. Six enemy dead were confirmed, and three AK-47 rifles and two rocket launchers with bombs were recovered.

* * *

Citation

Major Ramaswamy Parameswaran,
8 MAHAR (IC 32907)

On 25 November 1987, when Major Ramaswamy Parameswaran was returning from a search operation in Sri Lanka, late at night, his column was ambushed by a group of militants. With cool presence of mind, he encircled the militants from the rear and

charged into them, taking them completely by surprise. During the hand-to-hand combat, a militant shot him in the chest. Undaunted, Major Parameswaran snatched the rifle from the militant and shot him dead. Gravely wounded, he continued to give orders and inspired his command till he breathed his last. Five militants were killed and three rifles and two rocket launchers were recovered and the ambush was cleared.

Major Ramaswamy Parameswaran displayed the most conspicuous gallantry and thought nothing of dying at his post.

Gazette of India Notification
No. 9—Press/88

* * *

Character in Peace, Courage in War

No sacrifice is worth the name unless it is a joy. Sacrifice and a long face go ill together. Sacrifice is 'making sacred'.

– Mahatma Gandhi

Ramaswamy Parameswaran was born and brought up in Mumbai. Born on 13 September 1946 he studied at SIES High School and College. He was commissioned initially with 15 Mahar and subsequently joined 5 Mahar in January 1972 while they were fighting insurgency in the hills of Mizoram and Tripura.

Parameswaran's great assets were his qualities of character. All those he came in contact with, particularly the junior leaders he led and the troops he commanded speak of his 'quality leadership'. Although he was a highly disciplined and deeply committed officer and pushed himself to the limit, he was also a very thoughtful and considerate company commander. He led by personal example and never asked his subordinates to do anything he would not or could not do himself. The most difficult tasks found 'Parry Sahib', as he was affectionately called by his men, leading from the front.

Parameswaran was always found leading the most difficult patrols and the most dangerous missions. His favourite pastime would be to take a handful of men into the jungles and *Jhooms* (cleared stretches of forests) of Mizoram. Dominating his area of responsibility was something he not only preached but also practised. In consequence, even the most dogged and hardened insurgents kept away from his area for fear of being killed or captured. And yet he was kind and gentle with the local inhabitants. A simple, straightforward and uncomplicated man he was always happy and cheerful. He always put his juniors at ease. Seniority did not matter much to him—people did. He and his wife were very hospitable.

He received the news of his posting to 8 Mahar with joy, because he had heard that it was due to move to Sri Lanka. He accepted this new posting as yet another opportunity to live and fight with the men of his regiment.

Siachen Saga

The Struggle for Dominance on the World's Highest Battleground, 1987 to date

'Siachen' is a world apart. To those who have not been there, it would be difficult to conceive its beauty or to comprehend the brutal conditions under which men in uniform must continue to live and fight within its cold embrace. It is undoubtedly beautiful beyond words, in the pristine and primeval majesty of snow and rock and ice that cap the roof of the world.

Time has carefully marked its passing in the serrations that countless centuries have etched on ancient rocks that vary in every imaginable shade of brown and black, orange and indigo and within whose depths are concealed the fossils of living fish and plants and other aquatic organisms that were pushed up from beneath the sea in the awesome cataclysm that created the Himalayas millions of years ago. The snow and ice that cover these mountains—the icing of the cake, as it were—sparkle in scintillating hues of green and blue and white that make it breathtakingly beautiful. Breathtaking is apt because at these formidable heights there is not enough oxygen to even breathe. The Siachen Glacier is the second longest glacier in the world. Beneath the veneer of this bleak beauty lie menacing hazards that snatch away human lives if one is not careful. More lives are lost due to climate, crevasses, avalanches and altitude sickness than to fighting the war. Those who take these mountains lightly do so at their own peril. It was in such a world that Naib Subedar Bana Singh and his compatriots had to fight in defence of their motherland.

The Siachen area has unfortunately keen a bone of contention between Pakistan and India for many years. The dispute is 'unfortunate' because it could perhaps have been avoided. The cause goes back to 1949. In the Karachi Agreement of 1949, representatives of both nations drew the 'Ceasefire Line' across maps of Jammu and Kashmir from Manawar in the south, to Khor in the north and thence 'North to the glaciers' through NJ 9842. Presumably when they came up to this glaciated wilderness of snow and ice they stopped at grid point NJ 9842 on the presumption that neither side would be interested in contesting an area where not a blade of grass grows and even breathing is a problem.

Pakistan however complicated the issue subsequently: first, by illegally ceding some 5180 square kilometres of Indian territory to China in the area where the boundaries of India, Pakistan and China meet thereby altering the geo-strategic importance of this area; and second by permitting and assisting a series of foreign mountaineering and scientific expeditions in the area thus raising the issue of 'rights' in an area that did not belong to her. Being aware of the implications of the cartographic ambiguity of 1962, the devious nature of certain powers, and the turn events could take, the Indian Army became concerned at Pakistan activities in the area. Sometime in 1983 the Indian Army got wind of Pakistani plans to move physically into the area and in April 1984 took pre-emptive action and occupied the Saltoro Ridge which marks the western boundary of the glacier. Both sides now began jockeying for the occupation of an area of dominance in this harsh environment where climate, weather, ice and snow are more dangerous than enemy action. The episode which concerns us, that is, the action where Naib Subedar Bana Singh won his PVC goes back to 1987 when a spectacular misadventure was initiated by Pakistan when it ordered its troops to establish a post in Indian territory. A surreptitious raid was launched by a crack unit of the SSG (Special Service Group) to occupy a key peak in Indian territory on the Siachen Glacier which till then was not occupied by Indian troops. They named it 'Quaid Post' after Quaid-e-Azam Mohammad Ali Jinnah. To the Indian armed forces nothing is more sacred than safeguarding the integrity and sovereignty of the country. The occupation of this post in Indian territory was a challenge that could not be ignored.

Naib Subedar Bana Singh
8 JAMMU AND KASHMIR LIGHT INFANTRY

The Capture of Quaid Post by 8 Jammu and Kashmir Light Infantry

Quaid Post was located on a massive ice-mass known as Bila-fondla. This ice-mass rises very sharply and the post was located at an altitude of 21,153 feet above sea-level. The severity of altitude and climate is comparable to Mount Everest which is 29,028 feet high. At these heights the air is very rarified and the oxygen content very low. Winds with velocities of 40-60 kmph are normal and average temperatures range between -35 degrees to -55 degrees Celsius. At these temperatures icicles form beneath one's nose and nearly all liquids freeze.

The steep ice-wall of Quaid Post gives it a very dominating position and to defend it one has to just take potshots at anyone trying to crawl up. A number of attempts had been made by brave Indian troops but they had to be called off due to heavy casualties.

Naib Subedar Bana Singh came into his own when he volunteered to capture Quaid Post with four others who joined him in this endeavour. While other members of the battalion engaged the attention of Pakistani soldiers, Naib Subedar Bana Singh and his team slowly climbed and clawed their way up the steep wall of ice. The temperature that night was around -30 degrees Celsius, and the wind speed was very high. It had snowed incessantly the previous three days and the group at places had to wade through waist-deep soft snow. Due to the extreme cold the weapons of the support group were malfunctioning.

Taking advantage of the poor visibility due to heavy snowfall, Naib Subedar Bana Singh and his group managed to reach close to the enemy post. En route they crossed the frozen bodies of their comrades from their battalion, who had been killed in earlier attempts to capture the post. Just short of the objective Naib Subedar Bana Singh further divided his small group and using grenades rushed in. Lobbing grenades into the bunkers and finishing off the occupants with the bayonet, seven Pakistani SSG commandos were killed on the spot and the remainder fled. Naib Subedar Bana Singh was soon joined by others from his unit and the post was safe in Indian hands.

Naib Subedar Bana Singh was awarded the nation's highest gallantry award, the Param Vir Chakra for his daring action and the post was renamed 'Bana Top'.

* * *

Citation

Naib Subedar Bana Singh
8 JAK LI (JC 155825)

Naib Subedar Bana Singh volunteered to be a member of a task force constituted in June 1987 to clear an intrusion by an adversary in the Siachen Glacier area at an altitude of 21,000 feet. The post was virtually an impregnable glacier fortress with ice walls, 1500 feet high, on both sides. Naib Subedar Bana Singh led his men through an extremely difficult and hazardous route. He inspired them by his indomitable courage and leadership. The brave Naib Subedar and his men crawled and closed in on the adversary. Moving from trench to trench, lobbing hand grenades, and charging with the bayonet, he cleared the post of all intruders.

Naib Subedar Bana Singh displayed the most conspicuous gallantry and leadership under the most adverse conditions.

Gazette of India Notification
No. 9—Press/88

* * *

Who Dares Wins

No man has ever risen to the real stature of spiritual manhood until he has found that it is finer to serve somebody else than it is to serve himself.

– T. Woodrow Wilson

Bana Singh was born on 6 January 1949 in village Kadyal in Ranbir Singh Pura. He enrolled in the Army on 6 January 1969, his birthday. He was exactly 20 years old when he was enrolled.

Bana Singh hails from an agricultural family and he is the eldest of five brothers and three sisters. His father and mother are deeply religious and two of his brothers are both *ragis* (Sikh singers of sacred verses from the *Guru Granth Sahib*) in gurudwaras in Canada and the UK. He studied in the local village school till class VIII and thereafter took his matriculation examination in the neighbouring village of Badyal Brahma.

Bana Singh belongs to a family that is god-fearing and deeply religious and where character and integrity are of primary importance. Doing what was right came naturally to him. Simple and self-effacing, when asked by reporters to talk about the action that won him the Param Vir Chakra he said that any member of his battalion could have done what he did, but that somehow it fell to his lot to lead the team. At 5 feet 4 inches Naib Subedar Bana Singh, PVC stands tall.

Conclusion

■

After having studied these actions of our 'icons of courage', one cannot help but conclude that each and every one of them was working towards meeting a need larger than himself. Their actions are indicative of certain common traits: the ability to put the interests of others above their own, to do what they thought was right irrespective of the consequences; to do their duty towards their country and their countrymen in the face of certain death, and to respond with courage, well beyond the call of duty.

The mottos of the Indian Military Academy, Dehra Dun, and the National Defence Academy, Khadakvasla encapsulate these values. The motto of the Indian Military Academy, familiar to all those who have passed out through the portals of Chetwode Hall says it all: 'The safety, honour and welfare of your country come first always and everytime. The honour, welfare and comfort of the men you command come next. Your own ease, comfort and safety come last always and everytime.' The motto of the National Defence Academy sums this up in three words, 'Service Before Self.' However it is not only mottos that motivate. It takes more than a motto to lay one's life on the line, to sacrifice one's today for someone else's tomorrow. And that perhaps arises from a deep sense of values, of giving back to society more than one has received; of sharing a vision of tomorrow's world and making today worthwhile before handing it over as one's legacy to future generations.

To believe however that men of courage are without fear would be incorrect. Fear is common to all men. It is the conquest of fear that is the real heroism. Once combat commences, persons who lead, put away their personal feelings, and act instinctively as trained. Responsibility drives away personal apprehensions and one has to get on with the accomplishment of the mission. In the case of the jawan, the 'fellowship factor' takes over and this is the reason why so many fighting men sacrifice their own lives to save their comrades under fire.

When examining the factor of courage, one needs also to consider how soldiers face the fear of dying. In war, men face the probability of death daily and in so many ways, but they keep death away from their minds as best as they can. The young in particular feel that they can never die. They rationalise: 'I will not die till the bullet that has my name on it finds me.' This is a familiar belief behind which many avoid the thought of death. There are others who are fatalistic in another way and say: 'If you are to die, you will die and nothing can save you; and if you are to survive, nothing can kill you, so why worry?' There are yet others whose self-discipline and sense of duty are so strong that they are able to control fear in the execution of their duties. This is specially so amongst officers, because they are the ones who lead and need most to control fear, because fear like courage is contagious.

It is also important to understand that the fighting capacity of a soldier depends on how he is selected, trained and motivated. The nation that compromises on the 'quality' of its officers and soldiers does so at its own peril. Leadership also counts—values that political leaders stand for, and the generalship of the armed forces. The quality and effectiveness of operational plans and success in battle is what the soldier looks for in his senior officers, as also how they stand up to the pressure from politicians and bureaucrats to ensure that the Army gets what it needs, so that it can get on with its job.

Not to be forgotten is the place and honour that a nation

gives to its armed forces, which motivates a soldier to fight—pride in being a soldier; pride in wearing a uniform that signifies that he belongs to a select category of men that exists to protect the country's honour; privileged in belonging to a group that epitomises bravery, courage, gallantry, and chivalry and most of all secure in the knowledge that in the eyes of his countrymen, he matters. And therefore the manner in which a nation treats its soldiers is important. Does a nation remember its soldiers only in times of war? This is an area that needs attention.

In the ultimate analysis, it is courage that motivates the individual soldier to perform acts of gallantry beyond the call of duty—not because he has been ordered to do it, to carry out a difficult task involving a threat to his life, but because in his own mind he has decided to do what is right. Courage, therefore, as Lord Moran puts it, has its roots in character, and war is just another test in a soldier's life. And therefore men of character in peace are men of courage in war. We have seen what motivates courage, and it is upto the nation to do what it can to foster this battle-winning factor. Can a nation shape the character of its people? I believe it can, if it wishes to do so and thinks it is important enough! After all, a nation must know what it wants and also that it will only get what it strives for.

Mahatma Gandhi, the Father of the Nation, is perhaps the only political leader of our country who had some experience of war. He took part in the Boer War in South Africa as an ambulance assistant, and was a close witness to the horrors and vicissitudes of war. He said, 'A small body of determined spirits, fired by an unshakeable faith in their mission can alter the course of history.' The heroes of this story have shown us that courage has its roots in character. We need to build on this foundation to evolve a 'national character'. If we are able to do this, India will be truly great. If we don't, we shall be failing those heroes and ourselves, and the sacrifices made by them and the multitude of unknown soldiers would have been in vain. It is the courage of a few that inspires groups small or big to do great things—and because they are few, they need to be acknowledged, valued and honoured.

ANNEXURE I

Param Vir Chakra

For most conspicuous bravery or some daring or pre-eminent act or valour or self-sacrifice in presence of the enemy whether on land, at sea or in the air. The decoration may be awarded posthumously.

The Param Vir Chakra, the country's highest gallantry award, was instituted by the President on 26 January 1950 through *The Gazette of India*. The gazette laid down the following regulations effective 15 August 1947:

First: The decoration shall be in the form of a medal and styled and designated the Param Vir Chakra (hereinafter referred as the Chakra).

Second: The medal shall be circular in shape, made of bronze, one and three-eighth inches in diameter, and shall have embossed on the obverse, four replicas of Indra's *Vajra* with the state emblem embossed in the centre. On the reverse, it shall have embossed Param Vir Chakra, both in Hindi and English, with two lotus flowers between the inscriptions. A sealed pattern of the decoration shall be deposited and kept.

Third: The medal shall be suspended from the left breast by a plain purple-coloured ribbon of one and a quarter inches in width; on those occasions when only the ribbon is worn, a replica of Indra's Vajra in miniature shall be fixed in the centre of the ribbon.

Fourth: The Chakra shall be awarded for most conspicuous bravery, or some daring or pre-eminent act of valour or self-sacrifice, in the presence of the enemy, whether on land, at sea, or in the air.

Fifth: The Chakra may also be awarded posthumously.

Sixth: The distinction shall be conferred by the President.

Seventh: The names of those persons upon or on account of whom the decoration may be conferred shall be published in *The Gazette of India*, and a Register thereof kept under the directions of the President.

Eighth: The persons eligible for the decoration of the Chakra shall be:

(a) Officers and men and women of all ranks of Naval, Military and the Air Force, or any of the Reserve Forces, of the Territorial Army, Militia and of any other lawfully constituted armed force.

(b) Matrons, sisters, nurses, and the staff of the Nursing Services and other services pertaining to hospitals and nursing, and civilians of either sex serving regularly or temporarily under the orders of the above-mentioned forces.

Ninth: If any recipient of the Chakra shall again perform such an act of bravery as would have made him or her eligible to receive the Chakra, such further act of bravery shall be recorded by a bar to be attached to the ribbon by which the Chakra is suspended, and for every such additional act of bravery an additional bar shall be added, and any such bar or bars may also be awarded posthumously. For every bar awarded, a replica of Indra's *Vajra* in miniature shall be added to the ribbon when worn alone.

Tenth: The miniature decoration, which may be worn on certain occasions by those to whom the decoration is awarded, shall be half the size of the Chakra and a sealed pattern of the said miniature decoration shall be deposited and kept.

Eleventh: Every recipient of the Chakra being or ranking junior in rank to that of Sub-Lieutenant in the case of the Navy, Second Lieutenant in the case of the Army, and Pilot Officer in the case of the Air Force, shall, from the date of the act by which the decoration has been gained, be entitled to a special pension, and each additional bar shall carry with it additional pension for life at such rates as the

President may prescribe. On the death of the recipient of the Chakra to whom the clause applies, the pension shall be continued to his widow until her death or remarriage under such rules as may be prescribed by the President.

Twelfth: This Chakra shall rank first among all awards.

Thirteenth: The President may cancel and annul the award of the Chakra to any person together with any pension appertaining thereto not already paid, and thereupon his or her name in the register shall be erased and he or she shall be required to surrender his or her insignia; but it shall be competent for the President to restore the decoration when such cancellation and annulment has subsequently been withdrawn, and with it such pension as may have been forfeited.

Last: Notice of cancellation or restoration in every case shall be published in *The Gazette of India*.

Amendment

By an amendment dated 26 January1980, Clause 12 in the above regulation was deleted and the remaining clauses numbered accordingly.

Design of the Medal

The decoration shall be circular in shape, made of bronze, one and three-eighth inches in diameter, and on the obverse have four replicas of 'Indra's *Vajra*' with the State Emblem (including the motto) embossed in the centre which will be domed. On its reverse it will have embossed Param Vir Chakra, both in Hindi and English, with two lotus flowers between the text. The fitting shall be swivel mounted.

ANNEXURE II

Sardar Patel's Letter to
The Prime Minister
7 November 1950

My dear Jawaharlal,

Ever since my return from Allahabad and after the Cabinet meeting the same day which I had to attend at practically fifteen minutes notice and for which I regret I was not able to read all the papers, I have been anxiously thinking over the problem of Tibet and I thought I should share with you what is passing through my mind.

I have carefully gone through the correspondence between the External Affairs Ministry and our Ambassador in Peking and through him the Chinese Government. I have tried to pursue this correspondence as favourably to our Ambassador and the Chinese Government as possible, but I regret to say neither of them comes out well as a result of this study.

The Chinese Government has tried to delude us by professions of peaceful intentions. My own feeling is that at a crucial period they managed to instil into our Ambassador a false sense of confidence in their so-called desire to settle the Tibetan problem by peaceful means.

There can be no doubt that, during the period covered by this correspondence, the Chinese must have been concentrating for an onslaught on Tibet. The final action of the Chinese in my judgement, is little short of perfidy.

The tragedy of it is that the Tibetans put their faith in us, they chose to be guided by us; and we have not been able to get them out of the meshes of Chinese diplomacy or Chinese malevolence. From the latest position, it appears that we shall not be able to rescue the Dalai Lama.

Our Ambassador has been at great pains to find an explanation or justification for Chinese policy and actions. As the External Affairs

Ministry remarked in one of their telegrams, there was a lack of firmness and unnecessary apology in one or two representations that he made to the Chinese Government on our behalf. It is impossible to imagine any sensible person believing in the so-called threat to China from Anglo-American machinations in Tibet. Therefore, if the Chinese put faith in this, they must have distrusted us so completely as to have taken us as tools or stooges of Anglo-American diplomacy or strategy. This feeling, if genuinely entertained by the Chinese in spite of your direct approaches to them, indicates that, even though we regard ourselves as friends of China, the Chinese do not regard us as their friends. With the Communist mentality of 'Whoever is not with them being against them', this is a significant pointer of which we have to take due note.

During the last several months, outside the Russian camp, we have practically been alone in championing the cause of Chinese entry into the UNO and in securing from the Americans assurances on the question of Formosa. We have done everything we could to assuage Chinese feelings, to allay their apprehensions and to defend their legitimate claims, in our discussions and correspondence with America, Britain and the UNO. In spite of this, China is not convinced about our disinterestedness; it continues to regard us with suspicion and the whole psychology is one, at least outwardly, of scepticism perhaps, mixed with a little hostility.

I doubt whether we can go any further than we have done already to convince China of our good intentions, friendliness, and goodwill. In Peking we have an ambassador who is eminently suitable for putting across the friendly point of view. Even he seems to have failed to convert the Chinese. Their last telegram to us is an act of gross discourtesy not only in the summary way it disposes of our protest against the entry of Chinese forces into Tibet but also in the wild insinuation that our attitude is determined by foreign influences.

It looks as though it is not a friend speaking in that language but a potential enemy.

In the background of this, we have to consider what new situation faces us as a result of the disappearance of Tibet, as we know it, and the expansion of China almost up to our gates. Throughout history, we have seldom been worried about our north-east frontiers. The Himalayas have been regarded an impenetrable barrier against any threat from the North. We had a friendly Tibet which gave us no trouble. The Chinese were divided. They had their own domestic problems and never bothered us about our frontiers.

In 1914, we entered into a convention with Tibet which was not endorsed by the Chinese. We seem to have regarded Tibetan autonomy as extending to independent treaty relationship. Presumably, all that we required was Chinese counter-signature. The Chinese interpretation of suzerainty seems different. We can therefore, safely assume that very soon they will disown all the stipulations which Tibet has entered into with us in the past. That throws into the melting pot all frontier and commercial settlements with Tibet on which we have been functioning and acting during the last half century.

China is no longer divided. It is united and strong. All along the Himalayas in the north and north-east, we have, on our side of the frontier, a population ethnologically and culturally not different from the Mongoloids.

The undefined state of the frontier and existence on our side of a population with its affinities to Tibetans or Chinese have all the elements of potential trouble between China and ourselves. Recent and bitter history also tells us that Communism is no shield against imperialism and that Communists are as good or as bad imperialists as any other. Chinese ambitions in this respect not only cover Himalayan slopes on our side but also include important parts of Assam.

They have their ambitions in Burma also. Burma has the added difficulty that it has no McMahon Line round which to build up even a semblance of an agreement.

Chinese irredentism and Communist imperialism are different from the expansionism or imperialism of the Western powers. The former has a clock of ideology which makes it ten times more dangerous. In the guise of ideological expansion lie concealed racial, national and historical claims.

The danger from the north and north-east therefore, becomes both Communist and Imperialist. While our western and north-western threats are still as prominent as before, a new threat has developed from the north and north-east. Thus, for the first time after centuries, India's defence has to concentrate on two fronts simultaneously. Our defence measures have so far been based on the calculations of superiority over Pakistan.

In our calculations we shall now have to reckon with Communist China in the north and north-east—a Communist China which has definite ambitions and aims and which does not, in any way, seem friendly disposed towards us.

Let me also consider the political considerations on this potentially troublesome frontier. Our northern and north-eastern approaches consist of Nepal, Bhutan, Sikkim, Darjeeling and the tribal areas of Assam. From the point of view of communications they are weak spots. Continuous defensive lines do not exist. There is almost an unlimited scope for infiltration. Police protection is limited to a very small number of passes. There, too, our outposts do not seem to be fully manned.

The contact of these areas with us is, by no means, close and intimate. The people inhabiting these have no established loyalty or devotion to India. Even Darjeeling and Kalimpong areas are not free from pro-Mongoloid prejudices. During the last three years, we have not been able to make any appreciable approaches to the Nagas and the other hill tribes in Assam. European missionaries and other visitors had been in touch with them, but their influence was, in no way, friendly to India or Indians. In Sikkim, there was political ferment some time ago. It was quite possible that discontent is smouldering there. Bhutan is comparatively quiet, but its affinity would be a handicap. Nepal has a weak oligarchic regime based almost entirely on force; it is in conflict with a turbulent element of the population as well as with enlightened ideas of the modern age.

In these circumstances, to make people alive to the new danger or to make them defensively strong is a very difficult task indeed and that difficulty can be got over by enlightened firmness, strength, and clear line of policy. I am sure the Chinese and their source of inspiration, Soviet Russia, would not miss any opportunity of exploiting these weak spots, partly in support of their ideology and partly in support of their ambitions.

In my judgement therefore, the situation is one in which we cannot afford either to be complacent or vacillating. We must have a clear idea of what we wish to achieve and also of the methods by which we should achieve it. Any faltering or lack of decisiveness in formulating our objectives or in pursuing our policy to attain those objectives is bound to weaken us and increase the threats which are so evident.

Side by side with these external dangers we shall now have to face serious internal problems as well. I have already asked Iengar to send to the External Affairs Ministry a copy of the Intelligence Bureau's appreciation of these matters. Hitherto, the Communist Party of India has found some difficulty in contacting Communists abroad, or in getting supplies of arms, literature, etc., from them. They had to contend with difficult Burmese and Pakistan frontiers on the east or with the long seaboard.

They will now have a comparatively easy means of access to Chinese Communists and through them to other foreign Communists. Infiltration of spies, fifth columnists and Communists would be easier. Instead of having to deal with isolated Communist pockets in Telengana and Warangal we may have to deal with Communist threats to our northern and north-eastern frontiers where, for supplies of arms and ammunition, they can safely depend on Communist arsenals in China.

The whole situation thus raises a number of problems on which we must come to an early decision so that we can, as said earlier, formulate the objectives of our policy and decide the methods by which those actions will have to be fairly comprehensive involving not only our defence strategy and state of preparation but also problems of internal security to deal with which we have not a moment to lose. We shall also have to deal with administrative and political problems in the weak spots along the frontiers to which I have already referred.

It is, of course impossible for me to be exhaustive in setting out all these problems. I am, however, giving below some of the problems which in my opinion, require early solution and round which we have to build our administrative or military policies and measures to implement them.

(a)   A military and intelligence appreciation of the Chinese threat both on the frontier and to internal security.

(b)   An examination of our military position and such redisposition of our forces as might be necessary, particularly with the idea of guarding important routes or areas which are likely to be the subject of dispute.

(c)   An appraisal of the strength of our forces and, if necessary, reconsideration of our retrenchment plans for the army in the light of these new threats.

(d)   A long term consideration of our defence needs. My own feeling is that unless we assure our supplies of arms, ammunition, and armour, we would be making our defence perpetually weak and would not be able to stand up to the double threat of difficulties both from the west and north-west and north-east.

(e)   The question of Chinese entry into the UNO. In view of the rebuff
        which China has given us and the method which it has followed in
        dealing with Tibet, I am doubtful whether we can advocate its claims
        any longer. There would probably be a threat in the UNO virtually to
        outlaw China, in view of its active participation in the Korean war. We
        must determine our attitude on this question also.

(f)   The political and administrative steps which we should take to strengthen
        our northern and north-eastern frontiers. This would include the whole
        of the border i.e., Nepal, Bhutan, Sikkim, Darjeeling and the tribal
        territory in Assam.

(g)   Measures of internal security in the border areas as well as the states
        flanking those areas, such as Uttar Pradesh, Bihar, Bengal, and Assam.

(h)   Improvement of our communications, road, rail, air, and wireless, in
        these areas, and with the frontier outposts.

(i)   Policing and intelligence of frontier posts.

(j)   The future of our missions at Lhasa and the trade posts at Gyangtse and
        Yatung and the forces which we have in operation in Tibet to guard the
        trade routes.

(k)   The policy in regard to the McMahon Line.

These are some of the questions which occur to my mind. It is possible
that a consideration of these matters may lead us into wider questions
of our relationship with China, Russia, America, Britain and Burma.
This however, would be of a general nature, though some might be
basically very important, e.g., we might have to consider whether
we should not enter into closer relationship with Burma in order to
strengthen the latter in the dealings with China. I do not rule out the
possibility that, before applying pressure on us, China might apply
pressure on Burma. With Burma, the frontier is entirely undefended
and the Chinese territorial claims are more substantial. In its present
position, Burma might offer an easier problem for China and, therefore
might claim its first attention.

I suggest we meet early to have a general discussion on these
problems and decide on such steps as we might think to be immediately
necessary and direct quick examination of other problems with a view
to taking early measures to deal with them.

Vallabhai Patel
7 November 1950

ANNEXURE III

Miscellaneous Details About the PVC

Twenty-one personnel of the Armed Forces have so far been awarded the Param Vir Chakra, India's highest gallantry award. Of these, twenty are from the Army and one from the Air Force.

Miscellaneous details pertaining to the Regiment, Corps, States and Wars/Campaigns in relation to PVCs awarded are given below:

States		Defence Forces		Infantry Regiments	
Punjab	4	Army	20	Grenadiers	3
U.P.	4	Air Force	1	Sikh	2
H.P.	4			Kumaon	2
Rajasthan	2			J & K Rif	2
Haryana	1	**Regts/Corps of the Army**		Rajput	1
Maharashtra	1			Raj Rif	1
Delhi	1	Infantry	17	Guards	1
J & K	1	Armd Corps	2	Mahar	1
Tamil Nadu	1	Engineers	1	1 GR	1
Karnataka	1			8 GR	1
Bihar	1			11 GR	1
				8 JAK LI	1

Wars and Campaigns where PVCs have been awarded

Indo-Pakistan War 1947–48	5
UN Peacekeeping Operations, 1961	1
Sino-Indian War, 1962	3
Indo-Pakistan War, 1965	2
Indo-Pakistan War, 1971	4
Siachen 1987	1
Sri Lanka 1987	1
Kargil 1999	4

ANNEXURE IV

Equating British and Indian Highest Awards for Gallantry in the Field

Finding an equation between awards for gallantry in the field between Britain and India is not an easy exercise. Questions have however been asked and an answer seems necessary. An attempt is being made in this article, which is limited to only the highest award for gallantry in the field. This primarily concerns the Indian Order of Merit and its equation to the Victoria Cross and subsequently to the Param Vir Chakra.

Instituted in 1837 in three classes as the 'Order of Merit', the word 'Indian' was added to the title in 1903. It was awarded to officers and men of the Indian Army for acts of conspicuous gallantry in battle, and was considered to be the British Indian Army's equivalent to the Victoria Cross. Thomas Carter and W. H. Long in their authoritative book *War Medals of the British Army 1650-1891* reproduced in 1972 state: 'A similar decoration to the Victoria Cross called the Indian Order of Merit, is given to native officers and men of the Indian Army for personal bravery only. It is an eight-pointed star, having on a blue enamelled background, two crossed swords surmounted by the words "Reward for Valor" within a gilt laurel wreath. It is divided into three classes: the first, or senior star is gold, the second silver, and the third is also silver without the gilding. *Ribbon*: dark blue with red edges. The third class is to be obtained by any conspicuous act of gallantry on the part of any native officer or soldier in the field or in the attack or defence of fortified places. The second class is to be obtained by those who possess the third, and for similar services. The first class is to be obtained in like manner only by those who already possess the third and second classes. Every member of the Order of Merit is entitled to additional pay, and on his death his widow receives the allowance for three years.'

The award of the Indian Order of Merit, first class before 1911, in effect is the equivalent of having won the Victoria Cross with two bars. There is only one recorded case of an Indian soldier having performed an unprecedented fourth act of supreme valour for which he was awarded a gold bar to be worn with his first class IOM. This individual is Sub Krishanbir Nagarkoti, the 5th Gurkha Rifles (Frontier Force). See Annexure VII.

Queen Victoria on 29 January1856 who wished to reward 'Valour' by her fighting men in the Crimean War 1854–1856 instituted the Victoria Cross. It was not awarded to Indian officers and men. It was only in 1911 when King George V visited India, he announced that Indian soldiers were to be considered eligible for the Victoria Cross. Between 1911 and 1947, 40 Indian Army officers and men have won the Victoria Cross. (See Annexure VI). Accordingly the third class of the IOM was abolished in 1912. Indian Army soldiers awarded the IOM were admitted to the second class and subsequently to the first class for a second act of gallantry. The all-gold badge of the first class was also abolished at this time, future recipients receiving the equivalent of the old third class and second class medals on their being awarded the second and first class respectively.

In 1944 the IOM was reduced to a single class award, with a bar being instituted to recognise subsequent awards. Awards of the IOM bestowed between 1939 to 1947 had the words changed from 'Reward for Valor' to 'Reward for Gallantry'. The award of the IOM became obsolete with Indian independence on 15 August 1947. The newly instituted Param Vir Chakra on 26 January 1950 became India's highest award for gallantry in the field, the equivalent of the British Victoria Cross.

A comparative table is drawn up for easy understanding.

Comparative Table for the Highest Awards for Gallantry in the Field British and Indian Armies 1837–1950

	British Army	Indian Army
Between 1837 & 1856		Order of Merit in three classes
Between 1856 & 1903	VC	Order of Merit III Class
	VC and bar	Order of Merit II Class
	VC and two bars	Order of Merit I Class

Between 1903 & 1911   Nomenclature of the
                                        'Order of Merit'
                                        changed to 'Indian
                                        Order of Merit'

                      VC   Indian Order of Merit
                                        III Class
                      VC and bar   Indian Order of Merit
                                        II Class
                      VC and two bars   Indian Order of Merit
                                        I Class

Between 1911 & 1944   The VC becomes extensible to Indian soldiers with effect from 1911. The IOM Class III is abolished. The IOM Class I and II continue to be the most coveted award next to the VC. In 1939 the inscription on the medal was changed from 'Reward for Valor' to 'Reward for Gallantry'.

Between 1944 & 1947   IOM Class II abolished in 1944 and the IOM became a single class award with a bar for every additional act of gallantry. There were also some changes made to the design of the medal.

15 August 1947   IOM is abolished.

26 January 1950   VC   PVC

ANNEXURE V

List of PVC Awardees

1947–48

Major Somnath Sharma, 4 Kumaon, 3 November 1947, Badgam, Kashmir, (posthumous).

Naik Jadunath Singh, 1 Rajput, 13 October 1948, Naushera, Kashmir, (posthumous).

Company Havildar Major Piru Singh, 6 Rajputana Rifles, 17–18 July 1948, Tithwal, Kashmir, (posthumous).

Lance Naik Karam Singh, MM, 1 Sikh, 13 October 1948, Tithwal, Kashmir.

Second Lieutenant Rama Ragobha Rane, Bombay Engineers, 8 April 1948, Naushera – Rajauri, Kashmir.

1961

Captain G.S. Salaria, 3/1 Gorkha Rifles, 5 December 1961, Elizabethville, Katanga, Congo, (posthumous).

1962

Subedar Joginder Singh, 1 Sikh, 23 October 1962, Tongpenla, NEFA, (posthumous).

Major Shaitan Singh, 13 Kumaon, 18 November 1962, Rezangla, Ladakh, (posthumous).

Major Dhan Singh Thapa, 1/8 Gorkha Rifles, 20 October 1962, Ladakh.

1965

Company Quartermaster Havildar Abdul Hamid, 4 Grenadiers, 10 September 1965, Cheema, Khem Karan, (posthumous).

Lieutenant Colonel A.B. Tarapore, 17 Horse, 15 October 1965, Phillaura, Sialkot, Pakistan, (posthumous).

1971

Lance Naik Albert Ekka, 14 Guards, 3 December 1971, Gangasagar, Bangladesh, (posthumous).

Second Lieutenant Arun Khetarpal, 17 Horse, 16 December 1971, Jarpal, Shakargarh, Pakistan, (posthumous).

Major Hoshiar Singh, 3 Grenadiers, 17 December 1971, Basantar River, Shakargarh, Pakistan.

Flying Officer Nirmal Jit Singh Sekhon, 14 December 1971, Srinagar, Jammu and Kashmir (posthumous).

1987

Naib Subedar Bana Singh, 8 Jammu and Kashmir Light Infantry, 23 June 1987, Siachen Glacier, Jammu and Kashmir.

Major Ramaswamy Parameswaran, 8 Mahar, 25 November 1987, Sri Lanka, (posthumous).

1999

Captain Vikram Batra, 13 Jammu and Kashmir Rifles, 20 January 1999, Pt 5140, Dras/Kargil, Jammu and Kashmir, (posthumous).

Lieutenant Manoj Kumar Pandey, 1/11 Gorkha Rifles, 23 June 1999, Khaluber, Batalik, Kargil, Jammu and Kashmir (posthumous).

Grenadier Yogendra Singh Yadav, 18 Grenadiers, 4 July 1999, Tiger Hill, Kargil, Jammu and Kashmir.

Rifleman Sanjay Kumar, 13 Jammu and Kashmir Rifles, 4 July 1999, Flat Top Area, Kargil Area, Jammu and Kashmir.

ANNEXURE VI

Indian Recipients of the Victoria Cross

World War I

1. Sepoy (later Subedar) Khudadad Khan, 127 Baluchis, 31 October 1914.
2. Jemadar (later Subedar) Mir Dost, IOM, OBI, Sardar Bahadur, 55 Coke's Rifles (Frontier Force), 26 April 1915.
3. Naik Darwan Singh Negi, 1/39 Garhwal Rifles, 23/24 November 1914.
4. Lance Naik (later Jemadar) Lala, 1/41 Dogras, 21 January 1916.
5. Risaldar Badlu Singh, 14 Jat Lancers, 23 September 1918.
6. Lance Dafadar (later Risaldar) Gobind Singh, 28 Light Cavalry, 1 February 1917.
7. Rifleman Kulbir Thapa, 2/3 Gorkha Rifles, 25 September 1915.
8. Rifleman Gabar Singh Negi, Garhwal Rifles, 10 March 1915.
9. Naik (later Subedar) Shahamed Khan, 89 Punjabis, 12/13 April 1916.
10. Sepoy (later Lance Naik) Chatta Singh, 9 Bhopal Infantry, 13 January 1916.
11. Rifleman (later Naik) Karna Bahadur Rana, 2/3 Gurkha Rifles, 10 April 1918.

Waziristan

Sepoy (later Honorary Captain) Ishar Singh, 28 Punjabis, 10 April 1921.

World War II

1. Second Lieutenant (later Lieutenant General) P.S. Bhagat, Royal Bombay Sappers and Miners, July 1941.
2. Subedar Richpal Ram, 4/6 Rajputana Rifles, February 1941.

3. Havildar (later Honorary Captain) Parkash Singh, 5/8 Punjab Regiment, January 1943.

4. Subedar (later Subedar Major) Lalbahadur Thapa, 1/2 Gurkha Rifles, April 1943.

5. Company Havildar Major Chelu Ram, 4/6 Rajputana Rifles, April 1943.

6. Havildar (later Honorary Captain) Gaje Ghale, 2/5 Gurkha Rifles (Frontier Force), May 1943.

7. Naik (Later Jemadar, MVC) Nand Singh, 1/11 Sikh Regiment, March 1944.

8. Jemadar Abdul Hafiz, 3/9 Jat Regiment, April 1944.

9. Sepoy (later Subedar Major and Honorary Captain) Kamal Ram, 3/8 Punjab Regiment, May 1944.

10. Rifleman Ganju Lama, MM, 1/7 Gurkha Rifles, June 1944.

11. Naik (later Honorary Captain) Agan Singh Rai, 2/5 Gurkha Rifles (Frontier Force), June 1944.

12. Subedar Netrabahadur Thapa, 2/5 Gurkha Rifles (Frontier Force), June 1944.

13. Naik Yeshwant Gadge, 3/5 Maratha Light Infantry, July 1944.

14. Rifleman Tulbahadur Pun 3/6 Gorkha Rifles, June 1944.

15. Rifleman Sher Bahadur Thapa, 1/9 Gorkha Rifles, September 1944.

16. Subedar Ram Sarup Singh, 2/1 Punjab Regiment, October 1944.

17 Sepoy Bhandari Ram, 16/10 Baluch Regiment, November 1944.

18 Rifleman Thaman Gurung, 1/5 Gurkha Rifles (Frontier Force), November 1944.

19 Jemadar Parkash Singh, 14/13 Frontier Force Rifles, February 1945.

20 Lance Naik Sher Shah, 7/16 Punjab Regiment, January 1945.

21 Naik (Later Subedar major and Honorary Captain) Gian Singh, 4/15 Punjab Regiment, March 1945.

22 Naik Fazal Din, 7/10 Baluch Regiment, March 1945.

23 Rifleman Banbhagta Gurung, 3/2 Gorkha Rifles, March 1945.

24 Havildar Umrao Singh, Indian Artillery, December 1944.

25 Sepoy (Later Havildar and Honorary Naib Subedar) Namdeo Jadhav, Maratha Light Infantry, April 1945.

26 Lieutenant Karamjeet Singh Judge, 4/15 Punjab Regiment, March 1945.

27 Sepoy Ali Haider, 6/13 Frontier Force Rifles, April 1945.

28 Rifleman Lachhiman Gurung, 4/8 Gorkha Rifles, May 1945.

ANNEXURE VII

The Story of
Subedar Kishenbir Nagarkoti IOM

1212 Kishenbir Nagarkoti enlisted in the 5th Goorkha Regiment (the Hazara Goorkha Battalion) during the 1860s. He is first mentioned in the Regimental History for his gallantry during the 2nd Afghan War of 1878–1880 when his regiment was accorded its first Battle Honour, and particularly for his exploits in the battle of Monghyr Pass on 13 December 1878 when he was awarded the Indian Order of Merit (3rd Class). His campaign medals bear witness to his presence with the regiment throughout the war, including as they do, the 2nd Afghan War Medal with clasps Peiwar Kotal 1878, Charasia 1879, and Kabul 1879, together with the Kabul to Kandahar Star. It was for conspicuous gallantry at the battle of Charasia on 6 October 1879 that he gained the Indian Order of Merit (2nd Class). In action again at Kabul on 12 December 1879, and now promoted to Naik, he once again distinguished himself and by his courage and bravery won the Indian Order of Merit (1st Class).

On 18 June 1888, by which time Kishenbir Nagarkoti had risen through the ranks to Subedar, he accompanied a small force of the Oghi detachment of the 5th Goorkha Regiment commanded by Major Battye and comprising 58 rifles and 17 police on an expedition to the eastern slopes of the Black Mountain in the Agror area of the North West Frontier Province. The local Gujar tribesmen who constantly harassed the rear of the column resented the passage of the troops. Soon afterwards, Major Battye received a message that the Havildar in charge of the rear-guard had been wounded.

Accompanied by Subedar Nagarkoti, Major Battye retraced his steps in order to rescue the wounded Havildar but the main body, which was now out of sight, knew nothing about this. A stretcher was found for the wounded man but they had scarcely resumed their retirement when the tribesmen, with vastly superior numbers, pressed home their attack.

To cover the withdrawal of the stretcher party, only Major Battye, Captain Urmston of the 6th Punjab Infantry, who was unarmed, Subedar Nagarkoti, a Naik, three riflemen and a bugler were now left. Soon the tribesmen attacked this small party. One leaping from cover dealt Captain Urmston a blow with a hatchet. Another with a sword severely wounded Major Battye in the shoulder and left him grappling with his assailant. Subedar Nagarkoti then ran up and killed the assailant but with two wounded officers to protect, their retreat cut off, and their small number reduced by casualties, the plight of Subedar Nagarkoti's party was desperate. Here, however, Subedar Nagarkoti showed superb courage.

He urged his three remaining men to fight on and using his pistol, killed several of the enemy. Aided by his soldiers, soon reduced to two, he succeeded for a time in keeping the enemy at bay. The end came when Major Battye was killed—shot through the neck—and almost immediately afterwards Captain Urmston received a fatal wound. Surrounded as they were by tribesmen, Subedar Nagarkoti and his remaining two men could not recover the bodies but they managed to get away themselves and caught up with the main body in the village of Atir. Subedar Nagarkoti then led the whole detachment back to the scene of his last stand, recovered the bodies and commanded the return of the force to the safety of Oghi.

All three survivors of the rear-guard party gained awards for their bravery. Sepoys Indrabir Thapa and Motiram Thapa receiving the Indian Order of Merit (3rd Class) but an award for Subedar Kishenbir Nagarkoti was more difficult. He had already been admitted to the 3rd, 2nd and 1st Classes of the Order and initially it was doubtful if the government could confer any higher distinction. The problem was however solved by the Gazette announcement covering his award, which read:

'The Governor General in Council is pleased to sanction, as a special case, the grant to Subedar Kishenbir Nagarkoti, 1st Battalion, 5th goorkha Regiment, Punjab Frontier Force, of a gold bar, with the words "18th June 1888" inscribed thereon, to be attached to and worn with the Ribband of the decoration of the First Class of the Order of Merit, in recognition of his conspicuous gallantry on that date on the Black Mountain, Hazara, on which occasion, he, in company with two sepoys of the Regiment, bravely stood by and defended Major Battye and Captain Urmston from the attacks of a numerous body of the enemy.'

In 1892, Subedar Nagarkoti retired from the Army and went home to Nepal on pension at the age of 44. His achievements are unparalleled in the annals of the Indian Army.

His decorations and medals are proudly displayed, together with his portrait in oil by his regiment, now the 5th Gurkha Rifles (Frontier Force) in India.

Bibliography

Clarke, John D. *Gallantry Medals & Decorations of the World*, Pen and Sword Books Ltd., 2001.

Dalvi, Brigadier John. *Himalayan Blunder*, Orient Paperbacks, Hind Pocketbooks Pvt Ltd in arrangement with Thacker & Company Pvt Ltd Bombay.

Handout at the Investiture Ceremony, Param Vir Chakra, Government of India, New Delhi, January 2000.

Haynes, Edward S. 'The Evolution and Development of Representative Systems of Military Honour in India', Winthrop University (USA). Inaugural Lecture at the Centre for Armed Forces Historical Research, United Service Institution of India, 12 February, 2002.

Haynes, Edward S. 'The Decorations and Medals of the Republic of India', Orders & Medals Society of America.

India's Highest Gallantry Awards & the Men who won them, 1947 – 1995. Defence Review, New Delhi, 1995.

Jha, Prem Shankar. *Kashmir 1947-48*, Oxford University Press, New Delhi, 1998.

Kalkat, Major General O.S. *The Far Flung Frontiers*, Allied Publisher.

Moran, Lord. *Anatomy of Courage*.

Palit, Major General D.K., VrC. *War in the High Himalaya – The Indian Army in Crisis – 1962*, Lancer International, New Delhi, 1991.

Palsokar, Colonel R.D., MC. *Regimental History of the Grenadiers* and *Forefront Forever*, Regimental History, The Mahar Regiment.

Palsokar, Colonel R.D. *Red Pompoms: History of the Eighth Gorkha Rifles*, Commandant, Gorkha Training Centre, 1993.

Praval K.C. *Valour Triumphs*, Thomson Press.

Prasad, S.N. & Dharam Pal. *Operations in Jammu & Kashmir 1947-48*, Ministry of Defence, Government of India, New Delhi, 1987.

Rao, General KVK, PVSM. *Prepare or Perish*, Lancer Publishers, New Delhi, 1991

Sen, Brigadier L.P., DSO. *Slender was the Thread*, Orient Longman, Bombay, 1993.

Singh, Lieutenant General Hanut, MVC. *Fakhr-i-Hind, History of the Poona Horse.*
Singh, Major General Sukhwant, AVSM. *The Liberation of Bangladesh,* Vikas Publishing, New Delhi, 1981.

Search Engines/Internet

- *'Unknown Soldier'* Online Encyclopaedia, Microsoft-Encarta.
- *Gallantry Awards, Men of the IAF,* Bharat Rakshak.
- *The Indian behind the Param Vir Chakra,* google.com
- *'Heroism'* Bharat Rakshak

List of Commonly
Used Abbreviations

AC	Ashoka Chakra
Adm	Administration
CHM	Company Havildar Major
DSO	Distinguished Service Order
Engrs	Engineers
FF	Frontier Force
FFR	Frontier Force Rifles
GOC	General Officer Commanding
GR	Gorkha Rifles
Hav	Havildar
Hrs	Hours
IOM	Indian Order of Merit
J & K	Jammu and Kashmir
LMG	Light Machine Gun
L/Nk	Lance Naik
MC	Military Cross
MM	Military Medal
MMG	Medium Machine Gun
MBRL	Multi Barrel Rocket Launcher
Nk	Naik
Nb/Sub	Naib Subedar
Para	Parachute
PVC	Param Vir Chakra
UMG	Universal Machine Gun
Recce	Reconnaisance
2IC	Second-in-Command